# The Road to Democracy

# The Road to Democracy

## Taiwan's Pursuit of Identity

# Lee Teng-hui

PUBLISHED BY **PHP** INSTITUTE, INC.

*Note: Romanization and name order in this book follow country practice.*

Published by PHP Institute, Inc. Tokyo Head Office 3-10, Sanbancho, Chiyoda-ku, Tokyo 102 Japan; Kyoto Head Office 11 Kitanouchi-cho, Nishikujo, Minami-ku, Kyoto 601 Japan

Printed and bound in Japan by Toppan Printing Co., Ltd. Typesetting by Asahi Media International Corporation. Jacket design by Michiyoshi Gow. Book design and layout by Taniguchi Koitsu. The main text is set in 12-point Palatino.

First Edition, September 1999
ISBN4-569-60651-2

To the People of Taiwan

# CONTENTS

# *Preface*

F̲OR T̲AIWAN, 1998 was an eventful year in the realms of the economy, domestic politics, and foreign relations. Economically, we had to cope with the repercussions of the financial crisis that swept East and Southeast Asia, beginning with the plunge of the Thai baht in July 1997. Internationally, U.S. President Bill Clinton visited mainland China in June, and Mr. Jiang Zemin of the People's Republic of China went to Japan in November. These visits, plus the resumption of meetings between top-level business leaders on both sides of the Taiwan Strait, attracted close attention among the people of Taiwan as well as interested observers worldwide.

On the domestic political scene, in 1998 party politics further matured and competition among political parties intensified, a trend continuing since Taiwan's democratization program began in the early 1990s. Toward the end of the year, the "three in one" elections were held for the mayorship of Taipei and Kaohsiung, for municipal assemblies, and for the national legislature. Also, the public debate on regional security, begun in 1996, grew in intensity, taking on an increasingly realistic tone.

Under these rapidly changing circumstances, I continued to focus my efforts for democratization. In the fall, I set out on a series of campaign tours for the Nationalist Party's candidates in the three-in-one elections. As I stumped through the countryside, its beautiful landscapes and familiar terrain reminded me of my presidential campaign in 1996. Even more memorable were the crowds of enthusiastic supporters and the high expectations people placed in me.

It was during these hectic months of electioneering that I began to feel an urge to write a book for the people of Taiwan. After the three-in-one elections were over, I mulled a plan for the book for days, and finally began writing. It was exactly a year and seven months before my term as president would expire.

In planning this book I had several factors to consider and several objectives in mind. In the past ten years Taiwan has undergone unprecedented changes: democratization of its political system, diversification of its social fabric, and liberalization in many aspects of public life. In the aftermath of rapid institutional and organizational changes, the people of Taiwan are asking themselves, "Where are we headed?" and "What goals do we seek?" It is these questions I wanted to address in this book.

No one can tell what will happen tomorrow; perhaps only God knows. But with the twenty-first century so close at hand, we should make clear what our hopes are for the future of Taiwan and what we believe to be the right course of action to take from now on. Especially as president of the Republic of China on Taiwan and as a person who has single-mindedly pursued the realization of freedom and democracy in Taiwan, I feel it is my duty to present my own prescription for the Taiwan of tomorrow. I love Taiwan and its people and I want them to be confident and hopeful about their country's future.

I also hope that the messages contained in this volume will help my fellow Taiwanese identify their individual objectives in life, and know what it is they want to live for. It was partly with that aspiration that I briefly reviewed my own life at the beginning of the book—my childhood experiences, education, the process of my intellectual growth, and my quest for religious faith. That retrospective is also meant to be my humble response to the question, "Lord, where are you going?" (John, 13:36.)

Above all, I would like this book to contribute to a better, deeper understanding of Taiwan among people everywhere, in Taiwan itself, in mainland China, and throughout the world. To that end, I decided to have it published first in Chinese, and then in Japanese and English with technical assistance from PHP Institute, a think tank and publishing house headquartered in Kyoto, Japan.

In Chapter one, I talk about my family and my educational background in the context of Taiwan's modern history. I focus particularly on the cultural and intellectual influences I received in my youth and my later conversion to Christianity. I also discuss Dr. Sun Yat-sen's "Three Principles of the People," but a fuller exposition of my political philosophy is presented in Chapter two.

The survival of humankind in the twenty-first century will hinge on whether or not we can effectively control such "tectonic changes" as the rapid expansion of the market economy, the information and computer revolution, the aging of the population, dramatic advances in science and technology, polarization of the international power structure, and globalization of the economy. As a liberal democracy, Taiwan alone cannot remain aloof from this whirlpool of change. Its political leadership will be required to have keen insight into these worldwide trends and a broad vision of the future.

Situated at a crossroad in Asia, Taiwan must maintain complementary and cooperative relationships with the United States, Japan, mainland China, and other Asian countries, both economically and politically. How to create such a system in East Asia and make it work depends solely on the wisdom of the political leaders of the countries concerned. This behest is uppermost in my mind as I discuss Taiwan's domestic politics and economics and its relations with mainland China, the United States, and Japan in the next four chapters of this book.

The final chapter, "Taiwan in the Twenty-first Century," introduces the idea of the "new Taiwanese" that transcends the differences between those whose ancestors were indigenous inhabitants of the island, early immigrants from continental China, or more recent migrants to Taiwan during and after the Communist takeover of the mainland. The new Taiwanese must establish a clear self-identity in order to be the masters of their own destiny.

Taiwan still has a long way to go before it can become a mature liberal democracy and a truly affluent society. We will have to develop science and technology further, protect the environment, promote culture, and improve our social security programs. Problems abound for Taiwan, but I am confident that the new Taiwanese will continue to meet these challenges with courage and conviction after I leave office. The last section of Chapter seven, "When Lee Teng-hui Leaves " expresses my candid reflections about the future of Taiwan.

More than anything, I would appreciate reader responses to the present volume. Any comments, favorable or critical or neutral, will give me food for thought about the future of Taiwan and the remaining years of my life. I believe that cross-cultural dialogue and mutual understanding begin with the free exchange of honest opinions.

Finally, I would like to express my sincere gratitude to Mr. Eguchi Katsuhiko, Executive Vice President of PHP Institute, Inc. Without his encouragement and cooperation, neither the Japanese nor English edition of this book could have been published. Many persons on Mr. Eguchi's staff have been involved in the editorial and production processes, and I would like to thank them all for their respective contributions. The English version is a translation of the Japanese text, undertaken by Mr. Kano Tsutomu of the Center for Social Science Communication in Tokyo and his associates—Ms. Patricia Murray, Ms. Lynne E. Riggs, and Mr. Takechi Manabu. Dr. Linda L. C. Liu, Special Assistant to the President, Republic of China, carefully checked the translated text for corrections and suggestions. I value their conscientious work.

LEE TENG-HUI

September 3, 1999

# The Road to Democracy

# CHAPTER **1**

# My Intellectual
# and
# Spiritual Journey

$F$OR CENTURIES the people of Taiwan were denied the opportunity to govern themselves. No matter how hard they might strive, their homeland was not their own. Born in Taiwan in 1923, I too lived through the ordeal of a colonial people in my youth. Once, in a discussion with Japanese novelist Shiba Ryotaro (1923–96), I referred to "the pathos of being born Taiwanese," and this candidly spoken personal expression apparently shocked many, for the publication of this discussion in a major Japanese opinion journal stirred controversy. But I was simply being honest.

While its history is filled with the tragic and unfortunate, Taiwan itself is blessed in many ways—a warm, pleasant climate, diverse topography, and fertile soil. Taiwan is located far enough from the continent that it has been spared direct involvement in the internal strife and social unrest that frequently troubled the mainland. Yet it is near enough to have absorbed a wide variety of social institutions and cultural traditions from the continent, which were tailored to local needs and conditions.

### Growing Up in Colonial Taiwan

The earliest references to Taiwan in extant historical documents date from the third century. By the Ming dynasty (1368–1644), people from China's coastal areas began to migrate to the island and settle among the native inhabitants. It was a lush land of mountains rising steeply out of the cobalt-blue waters of the Pacific that sixteenth-century Portuguese explorers called "Ilha Formosa," or "beautiful isle." During the following century, the Dutch controlled Taiwan for a while until Cheng Ch'eng-kung, a general of the former Ming dynasty, expelled them in

1662. Twenty years later, the Cheng regime was toppled by the Ch'ing dynasty (1616–1912), which by then had replaced the Ming as the ruling dynasty.

Immigration from the coastal provinces of China accelerated during the Ch'ing dynasty until Taiwan came under Japanese control following the Sino-Japanese War (1894–95). Japan's colonial rule ended in 1945 with its defeat in World War II, and Taiwan once more became a province of China. Four years later, in 1949, the Kuomintang (KMT, Nationalist Party) relocated the capital of the Republic of China (ROC) to Taipei when the Chinese Communist Party (CCP) gained ascendancy on the mainland. The relocation of the Kuomintang government under President Chiang Kai-shek (1887–1975) not only brought Taiwan into a direct, tense relationship with the mainland across the Taiwan Strait but provoked friction between the descendants of early settlers, referred to as "Taiwanese," and the newcomers called "mainlanders."

Even this brief sketch suggests the complexity of Taiwan's history and the trials the people of Taiwan have had to endure. Perhaps because of, rather than in spite of, its tragic past, Taiwan has been able to nurture a unique culture rich in diversity, and its people have acquired the flexibility and adaptability with which to cope with adversity.

I believe that we are indebted to Taiwan and its recent history for our varied experience and exposure to different ways of thinking. Had I not been born in Taiwan, I would have been quite a different person in my values, in my outlook on life, and above all, in my experience of the world.

My ancestors came from mainland China and settled in Taiwan several generations back. As I mentioned earlier, Taiwan was a Japanese colony when I was born, hence I was educated in the prewar Japanese education system. I was fortunate enough to study at elite schools from primary through middle school, and then to go to higher school and one of the best universities in Japan. I entered Kyoto Imperial University in 1943 and studied agricultural economics. After the Pacific War ended, I returned to Taipei to complete my undergraduate work at National Taiwan University. Several years later, I did graduate studies at Iowa State University, and in the late 1960s I earned my doctoral degree in agricultural economics from Cornell University.

As this glance at my academic background shows, I had the rare opportunity to study in three vastly divergent cultural milieus. Not many young people are so lucky. The troubled history of modern Taiwan brought me this good fortune, so I feel I have an obligation to serve my society and to share what I have learned with my fellow Taiwanese.

## A Children's Encyclopedia

I have been blessed in my life. Born into a well-to-do family, I was able to study as much as I wanted. My father, Lee Chin-lung, was a graduate of the police institute and worked as a detective for about fifteen years. Among Taiwanese during the colonial period, police officers—along with school teachers trained at the local normal school—belonged to the elite. My mother, Lee Chiang-chin, was the daughter of a landowning village leader.

My father worked for the police long enough to be eligible for a pension, and upon his retirement, our family moved back to his hometown of Sanchih, where he served for some time as the chief of the village irrigation council and treasurer of the local agricultural association. After World War II ended, he became a member of the county legislature.

One problem with my father's official career was that it involved transfers from one post to another, which forced us children to change schools quite frequently. In fact, during my six years of primary school, I attended four different schools. It was impossible for me to make close friends when I was in one place for such a short period of time. Even when I did make friends, I had to leave as soon as I began to know them well and had to start all over again at the next school. This childhood experience had a significant effect on my personality, making me introverted and stubborn. Without friends to play with, I stayed home after school and on holidays, sketching things around me or reading books. Drawing exercises helped develop my skills in oil and watercolor painting and in woodblock printing, and these later became my major pastimes.

I was an avid reader, which made me far more "knowledgeable" than my peers. One of my boyhood treasures was *Jido hyakka jiten* [Encyclopedia for Children] published by Shogakukan in Tokyo. The story of how this Japanese encyclopedia came into my possession tells something about my father and his devotion to education.

When I was in fourth grade, our school organized an excursion to Taipei. On the night before our departure, I mustered up all my courage and went to see my father. Very hesitatingly, I said, "Father, I would like to buy a children's encyclopedia and a math book in Taipei. Together they come to about four yen. Do you think I can?" In those days (early 1930s), four yen was a big sum of money, perhaps 15 percent of my father's monthly salary on the police force. Far from getting angry with me, as I had feared, his expression turned sad, "Why didn't you tell me sooner what you wanted? I don't have that much money right now, and how can I scrape together such a large sum over-night!"

The next morning, before dawn, I and my classmates as-sembled near the Taoist shrine to get on a chartered bus. There was a light drizzle. My seat was in the second row from the front on the window side. We were almost ready to depart when I heard someone tap on my window. Turning, I saw a man hold-ing an umbrella. It was my father. He slipped me an envelope with the money through the bus window. Long before daybreak, he had somehow gathered the money from his friends. Years later, I often related this story to my own children. My father would listen quietly until I finished, and each time he would shake his head, smiling, and say, "I don't remember a thing about it."

## Yearning for Independence

In many ways my parents indulged me as a boy. They would do anything I asked. It was not just because they were financially well-to-do. My mother, especially, lavished me with love. Once I went swimming without telling her; she became extremely upset and unleashed a frantic scolding. I had to beg her forgiveness on my knees. She gave me preferential treatment at the dining table. Our family sold pork on the side, and we often had meat for dinner. I always found an extra portion on my plate.

Strange as it may seem, as I grew older I started to feel rebellious against my parents' indulgence and their almost smothering care. I always appreciated my mother's special attention, but I began to grow wary of it. I was afraid that I would end up being really spoiled.

I may have been a precocious child, and my intensive reading only accentuated my self-consciousness. Determined to resist my mother, I often insisted on having my own way, and my stubbornness would make her cry. She must have been at her wit's end in the face of my obstinacy and self-centeredness.

I had often begged to be allowed to live away from home. One day, I talked things over with my mother, and she agreed to the idea at long last. We decided that it was best for both of us. I transferred to a public primary school in the town of Tamsui and stayed with a friend's family and later at a teacher's house.

This experience of "independence" from my parents turned out to be very valuable, as it gave me the opportunity to learn much about human relations. I was made painfully aware of how dependent we are on other people's help. Living with people other than my own family made me more sensitive about my position in relation to others in any given situation. At meal times, for example, I had to think twice before asking for an extra helping.

## Japanese Thought

As my sense of self matured, I began to ask myself questions like "What does it mean to be human?" and "How should one live one's life?" This soul-searching started with something my mother said to me one day. "You are too easily swayed by emotion," she declared, and she advised me to try to use reason. After that I began to try to deal more rationally with the feelings that periodically exploded inside me.

In 1936 I entered Tamsui Middle School. By then, militarism was raging throughout the Japanese empire, affecting even secondary school education. As a refuge from the fanaticism that surrounded me, I read a great deal by Daisetz Suzuki, who interpreted the philosophy of Zen Buddhism from an international perspective. I was particularly impressed by the Zen concept of self-control.

Zen practice follows strict rules and principles of asceticism. The ascetic gets up before dawn and performs some form of physical labor, thereby cultivating a spirit of self-denial. The practice of standing under a cold waterfall is intended to bring one toward a state of perfect selflessness. Lin-chi I-hsüan (d. 867), the founder of the Zen sect in China, said that while the presence of thought gives rise to various phenomena, in the absence of thought various phenomena disappear. (*Lin-chi Lu* [Records of Lin-chi Teachings]). In other words, if you devote yourself totally to something, you lose yourself in the effort and you will not vacillate or waver in the path toward your goal.

Inspired by this strict spiritual discipline, I actively participated in early morning labor at my school dormitory. I devoted myself to cleaning the lavatories and to other menial chores that my classmates were unwilling to do. I always welcomed an opportunity to train myself in better self-control. This sort of asceticism was quite common among Japanese in those days. It was pervasive in the imperial army, affecting the thinking and behavior of the soldiers. Despite its sometimes negative consequences, there are some things about asceticism and the cultivation of spiritual strength that I believe are very important.

Besides Daisetz Suzuki's works, I read many books by other Japanese thinkers and men of letters, which played a large role in my intellectual development. Natsume Soseki (1867–1916), one of the most popular novelists in modern Japan, was my favorite. I read his collected works many times over. In my early adolescence I liked *Sanshiro* (1908) especially for its portrayal of a young man from the countryside who goes to study at the imperial university in Tokyo, and the agonies and hardships he experiences in his passage to adulthood.

*Santaro no nikki* [Santaro's Diary] (1914–15) by neo-Kantian philosopher Abe Jiro (1883–1959) was a best-seller among higher school students in the 1920s and 1930s. Abe's view that each person in his or her own way should try to live as fully as possible in order to find meaning and happiness in life struck a responsive chord. Another book I read over and over was *Shukke to sono deshi* [The Priest and His Disciples] (1916) by Kurata Hyakuzo (1891–1943). At the end is an account of the Buddhist priest Shinran (1173–1262), founder of the Jodo Shin sect. Just before he breathes his last he utters, "That is good. Everyone is saved... It is a good and harmonious world." This scene touched me profoundly. I felt that this remark encapsulated my ideal.

In addition to modern and contemporary works, I was also interested in Japanese classics, including the eighth-century *Kojiki* [Record of Ancient Matters], *Genji monogatari* [The Tale of Genji] (early eleventh century), *Makura-no-soshi* [The Pillow Book], and *Heike monogatari* [The Tale of the Heike]. My interest in *Kojiki* led me to read the great National Learning scholar of the Edo period, Motoori Norinaga (1730–1801), whose interpretative works on the Japanese classics are full of original insight into the essence of the culture. I especially liked his *Tamakatsuma*, a collection of more than one thousand essays.

Some readers may find it strange that a Chinese youth born in Taiwan was reading all these Japanese books. Actually, it was not surprising, since Taiwan was Japan's colony until August 1945 (when I was twenty-two years old), and I received a standard Japanese education. Naturally, Japanese books, classic and modern, were my primary source of knowledge.

I continued to read voraciously during my three years at Taipei Higher School. Apart from classical literature, my regular reading included *Zen no kenkyu* [A Study of Good] (1911) by philosopher Nishida Kitaro (1870–1945), *Fudo* [Climate and Culture] (1935) by philosopher Watsuji Tetsuro (1889–1960), *Arabia no Rorensu* [Lawrence of Arabia] (1935) by Nakano Yoshio, and a Japanese version of Albert Einstein's introduction to physics for lay people. I read these books so many times that the pages were worn to tatters, but I still keep them in my library.

Like the typical Japanese student of the time, I was also fond of Western works in translation, including *Sartor Resatus* by Thomas Carlyle (1795–1881), Goethe's *Faust* and *The Sorrows of Young Werther*, and Dostoevsky's *The Idiot*. In his never-ending quest for new light in the darkness of Russian society on the eve of revolution, Dostoevsky gave me much spiritual food for thought.

After the end of the second world war, there was a woeful shortage of books in Taiwan. Several of my friends and I brought our books together and opened a secondhand bookstore in Taipei. Our motivation, however, was to enlighten others rather than to operate a viable business.

## Chinese Culture Reconsidered

Although Japanese culture and education were the primary influences in my childhood, I also read extensively in Chinese philosophy and literature. I was particularly influenced by the currents of new thought that went back to anti-Japanese demonstrations and labor strikes of the May 4th Movement of 1919.

Chinese have always been proud of their long history, but after many centuries of feudalism China's traditional culture was misinterpreted and distorted, making social progress and reform extremely difficult. Hu Shih (1891–1962) was a pragmatist philosopher trained under John Dewey and a great literary critic. In an article written in 1928, "Mingchiao" [The Doctrine of Name], published in the journal *Hsinyueh*, Hu vehemently criticized the strong tendency in Chinese society to rely on slogans. The Chinese people do not have religious faith, he declared; instead they are very superstitious and blindly follow the traditional teaching that equates "name" (i.e., word) with "reality." They literally "worship the religion of the written word," thereby failing to face reality squarely and turning to slogans (i.e., words) for their psychological satisfaction. The net result is, according to Hu Shih, the failure to resolve real problems in the world and the tendency to pervert value. He called on the political leaders of his time to stay away from slogans and put their words into practice in governing the country.

In *The True Story of Ah-Q* and other works, Lu Hsun (1881–1936) satirized "the preoccupation of Chinese people with saving face." His novels won the sympathy of many readers, including myself. Lu Hsun argued that Chinese never bothered to solve problems but rather sought their own comfort and tried to save face. Such an attitude, he asserted, was what caused Chinese society to stagnate and fail to change with the times.

The historian Kuo Mo-juo (1893–1978) was another writer who harshly criticized Chinese feudalism and urged the youth of his day to stand up for social reform. His *Ten-point Criticisms* and *The Bronze Age*, among others, evaluate pre-Ch'in thinkers and their ideas. While he valued the philosophies of Confucius and Mencius for their democratic ideas, Kuo rejected Han Fei tzu's notions of the rule of law and monarchism, as well as Ch'in Shih-huang-ti's extreme authoritarianism. China could develop, Kuo argued, only by promoting democratic ideals and by freeing itself from the fetters of tradition.

These works critical of China's traditional society evoked far-reaching responses among the educated Chinese youth of the day. I was in my early twenties when I studied these books and pondered the problems of Chinese culture. Feudalism, I realized, was the biggest barrier to China's modernization and the cause of its stagnation. It seemed to me that Chinese thought and behavioral patterns, too, had been affected by the adverse social conditions it imposed.

I have tremendous respect for the Chinese thinkers who tried to enlighten their countrymen in the 1930s. But society then was neither mature enough to heed their advice and warnings, nor determined to look to viable solutions for the problems at hand. Many young Chinese aspired to revolutionary ideals, but they had no clear vision of what they sought nor any well-marked path to follow.

What we see in Taiwan today is, in a sense, the result of implementing reformist ideas from the 1920s and early 1930s. For the past decade or so, we have enjoyed stable economic and social development, and in the process we have gradually been able to cast off the fetters of tradition. Through extensive social and political reforms, Taiwanese society has achieved a new level of maturity. Needless to say, we still have a long way to go before we can approach our ideals through further reform. But I am convinced that the road we have taken is the right one, and that our achievements demonstrate that the revitalization of Chinese culture is indeed possible.

For some time now, I have been talking about the need for "renewal of the spirit." This kind of reform goes deeper and is much harder to carry out than political or institutional reforms. Yet it is vital if Taiwan is to throw off its outmoded cloak and plunge into a new era of dynamic development. Only when people equip themselves with modern values, a rational way of thinking, and a democratic mindset will Taiwan become a truly free, open society. Our goal is to make Taiwan a new center of Chinese culture built on the principles of freedom, democracy, and internationalism.

## The Lure of Marxism

In April 1943 I entered the Faculty of Agriculture at Kyoto Imperial University. A variety of factors influenced my decision to major in agricultural economics. One was my childhood experience. During the mid-summer and year-end holidays I often saw farmers who worked my family's land come to our home with gifts, pleading that their tenancy be continued. Though still a young boy, I wondered why these farmers had to be so subservient. "They are human beings no different from my father, but what or who makes them behave like servants?" I asked myself with indignation. I noticed with particular interest that there were substantial differences in productivity and per-acre harvest from one tenant to another.

A Chinese history course I took in higher school also motivated me to study agricultural economics. Professor Shiomi Kaoru was a Marxist historian, and his interpretation of Chinese history had a strong impact on my understanding of social structure. By the time I finished higher school, the combined influence of my boyhood experiences, Marxist economics, and my realization of the importance of agriculture to Taiwan's future led me to decide to specialize in agricultural economics.

While a student at Kyoto Imperial University, I read everything I could get my hands on by Karl Marx and Friedrich Engels, from their early treatises all the way to *Das Kapital*. I clandestinely read Marx's multi-volume masterpiece a number of times in Japanese translation. In wartime Japan one risked arrest and duress by the Special Thought Police if caught carrying or possessing any Marxist or socialist literature. I was nevertheless attracted by Marxist economics, not only because it was based on a philosophy of liberation but because it focused on an analysis of capital.

Even today, economists tend to dwell on the relationship between production and distribution in the context of the market mechanism, primarily from the standpoint of flow rather than stock. Stock is more relevant, however, when you are concerned about the takeoff stage of an economy and its development to the stage of maturity. In *Das Kapital*, Marx approached economics from the perspective of stock and tried to clarify exactly what capital is. He explained that if "reproduction" is accompanied by the expansion of production and consumption, this "reproduction on an enlarged scale" makes accumulation of capital possible. If, on the other hand, the level of production remains constant, it will be only "simple reproduction" with no capital accumulation, and society will cease to develop.

Up to this point, Marxian economics made sense to me; the fundamental differences between the two types of reproduction were especially relevant to my concern for the future of Taiwan's economy. But the problem was that the Marxist theory of reproduction is conceptual, and therefore not quantitative. No matter how valid or useful a theory, it cannot be applied in economic analysis unless it is somehow quantifiable.

Another basic complaint I had about Marxism was its negative view of Asia. Marx himself inherited from Hegel the idea that Asia was backward and stagnant. The so-called Asiatic mode of production was a stumbling block to such later Marxists as Nikolai Lenin and Karl J. Kautsky as well. In the 1930s Karl Wittfogel, a German-born sociologist and Sinologist, came up with a more sensitive analysis of the problem in his *Theorie der Orientalischen Gesellschaft* (1938). He found a relationship between Asian paddy field agriculture, namely wet rice cultivation, and "Oriental despotism." On the whole, however, European Marxism omitted "backward Asia" from its analysis.

## A Peasant Revolution?

It was none other than Mao Zedong who tackled this troublesome problem by arguing that the Chinese revolution should be centered on the peasantry, as opposed to the proletariat (i.e., labor) in the case of a European revolution. Had a genuine peasant revolution been carried out in mainland China, it would have been a major breakthrough in Chinese history. In actuality, however, such a revolution did not take place in China even under Mao's leadership. For any peasant revolution to be truly meaningful, it must increase the productivity of limited arable land. To accomplish this, it must include an agricultural reform that eases the exploitative relationship between landowners and land cultivators, thereby giving farmers greater motivation to work. In other words, agricultural reform must encompass an improvement of the land tenancy relationship, in addition to developing agricultural technologies and establishing agricultural extension systems. After all, raising agricultural productivity is the ultimate purpose and priority of a peasant revolution.

From my point of view, Mao Zedong's biggest mistake lay in embracing typical Chinese paternalism and the dictatorship to which it led. He used political class-struggle methods to transform the land tenancy relationship and instituted the "people's communes" to maintain control over the peasantry. Mao did not give individual farmers the opportunity to develop agricultural extension strategies or better agricultural techniques. The peasant revolution therefore failed to achieve its ultimate purpose or goal. Even today, Communist China has not succeeded in improving agricultural productivity; it still does not produce sufficient food and grain to feed its entire population.

Mao never relinquished his dictatorial power. The Cultural Revolution was a case in point. It was a prime example of his style of power politics used in an attempt to retain absolute authority. But as long as political power remained concentrated in the hands of one individual, a new page in Chinese history could never be turned.

Today, Peking is trying to strengthen its relations with Washington, but its basic pattern of behavior has not changed at all. It appears to be conducting "great power diplomacy" vis-à-vis the United States, but in reality it is simply trying to erode America's political and economic base in Asia. In no way is mainland China a great power capable of competing with the United States. Its only resource is its huge population. If mainland China ever perceives that it has taken over a substantial portion of the American base in Asia, it will abandon its policy of following the U.S.

lead and switch to a policy of weakening, and then driving out, the American presence from the region.

Let me now go back to my student days. Having been so engrossed in Marxist economics, I seriously wanted to write my graduation thesis on "The Problem of Agriculture in Taiwan under Japanese Imperialism." But that was too controversial a topic in those days, so I changed the title to "A Study on the Problem of Farm Labor in Taiwan." Regardless of the theme, my intention was to employ Marxist economics to analyze the agricultural industry of Taiwan in terms of class issues.

## From Marxism to Christianity

When World War II ended in August 1945, I was in Nagoya serving as a second lieutenant in the Imperial Japanese Army. Like many other university students in Japan I had been mobilized for military service. I was torn between continuing my studies at Kyoto Imperial University or going back to Taiwan. In the spring of 1946, I returned to Taiwan and was enrolled at National Taiwan University (Taipei Imperial University under the Japanese system).

At this point, I must touch on the February 28 Incident of 1947, for it sheds light on the early postwar phase of my intellectual journey. In a nutshell, the incident was a case of the severe oppression of Taiwanese by the KMT government. What really complicated the incident was that it triggered a series of "white terrorist" attacks against Taiwan-born intellectuals, whom the KMT authorities unilaterally labeled "Communists."

Taiwan's postwar history began in October 1945 with the abolition of Japan's Government-General in Taipei, but the island was soon caught in the middle of a fierce struggle for power between the Nationalists and Communists. As the tide of war on the mainland turned against the KMT, the Nationalists were forced to fall back to Taiwan, where they intensified their authoritarian control over the local population.

It all started on February 27, 1947, with a minor incident that occurred in the shopping district along the Tamsui river running through the city of Taipei. Trouble quickly flared into a protest movement by the local Taiwanese. The provincial governor Chen Yi then asked Generalissimo Chiang Kai-shek for reinforcements, and that was to lead to real tragedy.

A contingent of about 13,000 reinforcements landed at the port of Keelung on March 8 and immediately began killing local protesters and arresting their leaders. Arrests and slaughter were extensive. Intellectuals believed to be potentially antagonistic to the KMT became special targets; they were either murdered or put in jail almost indiscriminately. There were probably no less than 30,000 victims. Many years later, shortly after I assumed the presidency of the Republic of China, I offered apologies to the victims of the February 28 Incident and actively pushed forward the payment of compensation to them or their families.

But, where was I at the time of this tragic incident? Still a student at National Taiwan University, I was, of course, on the side of the oppressed. I could not have just shut myself up in my study and turned a deaf ear to the tragedies taking place right under my nose. As I was a passionate young man keenly concerned about the future of Taiwan, I responded to the urging of fellow students and, on a few occasions, attended a study group that examined the liberal economic and socio-political ideologies of the day. Not finding the discussions particularly stimulating, however, I soon stopped going. In the frenzy and chaos following the February 28 Incident, several of the students and teachers who had participated in the study group were either arrested, killed, put on a blacklist, or became the target of surveillance and interrogation. In those times, one often heard of a teacher, friend, neighbor, or acquaintance suddenly being taken into custody or disappearing, never to be seen again because they had become fugitives, were arrested, or were killed. One day in 1969, I was suddenly woken up in the middle of the night and taken away by the Taiwan Garrison Command for several consecutive nights and days of interrogation. I learned then that I had been under the surveillance of the secret police since the February 28 Incident. When I mentioned this in 1994, leaders of the opposition party criticized me, saying "That couldn't have been true." But those people were not even born in 1947. They have no way of knowing what really happened and how certain individuals reacted to the incident. Only the ones who lived through those difficult times can testify to their feelings and actions.

In any case, two years and a half after the February 28 Incident, the Nationalist government left the mainland to relocate the capital of the Republic of China in Taipei. Beginning in August 1949, Taiwan entered a new era of direct rule by Generalissimo Chiang Kai-shek.

I found a teaching job at my alma mater, married, and even

went to the United States for advanced study. Several years passed and I began to feel the emptiness of a life dedicated to the pursuit of nothing but knowledge. I realized that I could no longer carry on my pursuit of only the reasoned and rational. Many things in this world defy rational explanations. Deep inside me, I felt a yearning for religious faith, the belief in some transcendental being.

No matter how unbearable life is, ennui does not lead one straight to belief in God. In our case, my wife and I finally converted to Christianity only after many years of serious soul-searching and listening to countless sermons by clergymen. Upon our return from Iowa in 1953, we made the rounds of all the different Christian churches in Taipei for three years, attending three or four services a week. At each church, we talked with the minister or priest, asking all sorts of questions centering on the reality of God.

Embracing faith is a very difficult thing to do. Scientifically, it is impossible to accept the idea, for example, that Mary conceived a child as a virgin. But Christianity tells you to believe it. The story of Jesus's resurrection is also beyond common sense. But again, for Christians, it is a cardinal article of faith.

### Believing the Invisible

From my own experience, you begin to appreciate the importance of believing in something beyond reason or comprehension when your established frame of reference collapses or is pulled out from under you. Bigoted intellectuals find it especially hard to embrace faith for fear of losing their grip on reality. It takes time and some extraordinary experience to overcome the mental barrier to unconditional faith.

I have read the Bible from cover to cover many times, both the Old and New Testament. One section that has left an indelible impression on me is the story about Doubting Thomas in the Gospel of John.

> One of the Twelve, Thomas, that is the "Twin," was not with the rest when Jesus came. So the disciples told him, "We have seen the Lord." He said, "Unless I see the mark of the nails on his hands, unless I put my finger into the place where the nails were, and my hand into his side, I will not believe it."
>
> A week later his disciples were again in the room, and Thomas was with them. Although the doors were locked, Jesus came and stood among them, saying, "Peace be with you!" Then he said to Thomas, "Reach your finger here, see my hands. Reach your hand here and put it into my side. Be unbelieving no longer, but believe." Thomas said, "My Lord and my God!" Jesus said, "Because you have seen me you have found faith. Happy are they who never saw me and yet have found faith." (John, 20: 24-29)

If you believe something simply because you have seen it, that is not real faith. We cannot see what is in someone else's heart, but we know that it is there. By the same logic, belief in God does not depend on his visibility or on proof of his presence. God is invisible, but he exists if you believe he does.

The greatest thing I have learned from Christianity is the idea of love. To me, the Christian concept of love boils down to taking an affirmative view of life. Among the great thinkers in history are many who tried to look back on their lives in a positive light. The priest Shinran, mentioned earlier, is one. The ultimate aspiration even of Friedrich Nietzsche, well known for his "God is dead" thesis, was in his later years to live "a life to which I can say 'ja'!"

Affirmation of faith in life is the central theme of Goethe's *Faust*. At the outset of this great drama, Doktor Faust enters into a contract with Mephistopheles in which the scholar wagers his soul in the conviction that he can never be satisfied with this life—that there would never be a moment in which he will say, "Ah, tarry still! thou art so fair!" But there is such a moment, and when Mephistopheles comes to claim his soul, he finds that Faust's sins are purified and his soul is being guided to heaven by angels.

Goethe's message here is an affirmation of the infinite depth of the love with which God saves those who have lived a life of earnest striving, no matter how sinful they have been. Goethe himself served as chief minister in the principality of Weimar. His image of the ideal state and his actual experience as a statesman might have overlapped with Faust's adventurous life in the "great world."

My own paraphrase of Goethe's message is that humans are all egotistic individuals, but insofar as we are members of society we must live with love for each other. If that spirit of love is deep and affirmative enough to manifest divine love, society will be filled with compassion and vitality. This conviction is at the core of my political philosophy and underlies my basic stance as a political leader.

Let me say a few words here about the differences between Christianity and Confucianism, which is very much a part of traditional Chinese culture. Sorely lacking in Confucianism are teachings that address "death" and "resurrection." These are important homologous concepts in Christianity, and I believe their absence in Chinese thought has been a basic source of many social problems.

The Analects of Confucius contain teachings that certainly express an affirmative view of life. However, there is no moment of negation in Confucius' outlook on life, as shown by his statement, "I yet know nothing of life. How can I know about death?" Inherent in Confucian philosophy, therefore, is the danger of overemphasizing the positive aspects of life.

Meaningful "life" deserves affirmation, but "life" and "death" are two sides of the same coin. We cannot live in a meaningful way unless we are constantly aware of the possibility of dying. Here, however, dying does not mean the end of physical life only, but the negation of self.

Goethe has a line in West-östlicher Divan (1819) that is more terse, more direct than similar verses in Faust: "Die, and become yourself." In other words, a truly affirmative "life" is possible only through the "death" of the self.

### The Purpose of Studying *I Ching*

In embracing Christianity, I broke new ground in my study of the meaning of life, and the faith had great impact upon my thought, speech, and actions. Being baptized was a major turning-point in my life. Later on, however, I entered politics quite unexpectedly and became president of the Republic of China, finding myself in a world of kaleidoscopic change. Wanting to get a clear view of what was going on and to understand the essence of change, I was seized by a strong urge to study *I Ching* [The Book of Changes], one of the basic Chinese classics.

By chance I came across a book, *I Ching and Modern Life*, written by Liu Chun-tsu, which further deepened my interest in this ancient philosophy. For about a year beginning in August 1994, I received weekly instruction on *I Ching* from Mr. Liu.

My purpose in studying this book was not to learn how to tell fortunes or plan my life. A head of state must know how to deal with situations at home and overseas that are changing every day. In making policy decisions that take into account the process of change, a political leader has to discern the facts behind the phenomena, see events in their proper perspective, and set priorities. The optimal policy for a state and its people should be determined according to such judgments. This is the most important role a national leader can play. I wanted to have a better grasp of government and policymaking via a greater understanding of the unchangeable essence of phenomena through research on the principle of *i*.

*I* is an equation of time. It can be explained by the three concepts of *pien-i*, *chien-i*, and *pu-i*. These correspond to the three truths of Buddhism: *pien-i* to "all things are impermanent"; *chien-i* to "all elements are nonsubstantial"; and *pu-i* to "nirvana is quiescence." Stated more plainly, *I Ching* teaches that "Time never stops changing, and all things in the universe change accordingly. In constant change there exists unchangeable truth. In order to understand the unchangeable essence of things and predict [phenomenal] change, one must have a sincere spirit."

The symbols used are simple. The two cosmic forces are represented by a divided line (-- --) for the *yin* (passive element) and an undivided line (—) for the *yang* (active element). The temporal and spatial interaction of heaven, earth, humanity, beginning, flourishing, and ending generates eight trigrams. After one cycle ends, a new cycle begins. The eight trigrams multiply to become sixty-four hexagrams, representing all possible forms of change and correlation among things in the universe.

By studying the principle of changes, I acquired a new understanding of the complex relations among human beings, between human beings and organizations, and among organizations. At the same time, I found many valuable hints about the ego, relations between humanity and institutions, activity in the international community, and problems involving national leadership. This newfound understanding led to my emphasis on "harmony" and "managing great Taiwan, establishing a new center of culture."

In the course of seeking the principle of changes, I acquired a better grasp of the traditional Chinese philosophical concept of humanism (*jenpen*). Many people in Asia believe that democracy and freedom are imported concepts. A close look at the history of Chinese thought, however, reveals an ancient indigenous respect for these values in the work of Confucian scholars who attached importance to liberty and humanism from long ago. Later, as China fell deeper into the thrall of centuries of feudalism, the native concept of humanism was increasingly distorted.

My examination of classical Chinese thought further strengthened my commitment to carrying out democratic reforms. Despite the obstacles, I have continued to initiate constitutional reform and implement democracy over the past decade precisely because of my conviction that democracy is a necessary process for the advancement of civilization and a value that should be shared by all people. Regardless of differences in locale, culture, or tradition, democracy is universal. I consider it my most important work as the head of the Republic of China to build a democratic society where all the people of Taiwan can fully express their individuality and lead happy lives.

### The Three Principles of the People

Another important source of inspiration for my political philosophy is Sun Yat-sen's Three Principles of the People. His motto, "The world is for all," written in Chinese calligraphy and framed, hangs on the wall of my office. These words form the core of my political beliefs.

Sun Yat-sen's motto parallels the Preamble of the Republic of China's 1947 Constitution, as well as the provision in Article I of that document. The Preamble reads, "We do hereby establish this Constitution in order to consolidate the authority of the state, safeguard the rights of the people, ensure social tranquility, and promote the welfare of people in accordance with the teachings bequeathed by Dr. Sun Yat-sen in founding the Republic of China."

Article I of the 1947 national charter reads, "The Republic of China, founded on the Three Principles of the People, shall be a democratic republic of the people, to be governed by the people, and for the people."

Sun Yat-sen espoused the Three Principles of the People as the ideological underpinning for the Nationalist revolution of 1912. The theory behind the three principles may be summed up in the following way:

> What is necessary for China today is to bring down the autocratic government of the Ch'ing dynasty, liberate the country from invasion by imperialists, and build a China of the Chinese people. The new China must be a democratic republic, not an autocratic monarchy.
>
> To these ends, we initially assumed that nationalism and popular rights were sufficient. We now realize that even in Europe where democratic revolutions have already taken place, the people's livelihood has not improved at all. This is behind the movements for social revolution there. Although there is no need for a social revolution in China today, we must anticipate the rise of social problems as we accomplish our democratic revolution. We should not try to solve such problems all at once. We must uphold the principle of the people's welfare even as we champion nationalism and popular rights.

**Nationalism, Popular Rights, and Welfare**

I studied the Three Principles of the People for the first time in my higher school days. A Japanese translation of Dr. Sun's book had been published by Kaizosha in Tokyo. I also read President Chiang Kai-shek's *Destiny of China* in Japanese before World War II began.

In both these books, the authors expressed concern about the serious social problems in China. As a higher school student, I was particularly interested in the insights on the problems of Chinese history, society, politics, and culture in these books.

Even now I remain impressed by Sun Yat-sen's outstanding Three Principles of the People ideology, because he had the vision to emphasize the people's rights. I admire his firm commitment to the idea that "the world is for all." It is these two ideas that the Chinese people have failed to embrace. Too often they act selfishly, stubbornly guarding their individual interests at the expense of social harmony.

In mainland China today the principle of people's rights and the idea that the world exists for all are conspicuous by their absence. Nationalism, combined with hegemony, is instead given first priority among the three principles by the People's Republic of China. I am wary of such a hegemonic attitude, for it is potentially very dangerous.

Whenever we think about nationalism in the Three Principles of the People, we should be careful not to remove it from its historical context. Sun Yat-sen, we must remember, propounded his Three Principles when European imperialism was still vigorous. Under such circumstances, he considered nationalism vital in securing the democratic rights of the people.

### An Accurate Grasp of the Land Problem

Sun Yat-sen also had an accurate understanding of the land problem. As an agricultural economist, I cannot but admire his thorough grasp of such a complex matter.

In classical economics as well as Marxism, land is not treated as an ordinary commodity but as property, a natural resource to produce "absolute rent." By contrast, modern and contemporary economists make no distinction between land and other commodities. To them, land is in abundant supply and can be easily purchased by locals and foreigners alike; therefore, land is deemed a commodity.

But farmland cannot be treated so simplistically. The location of a particular plot of land is a crucial factor that cannot be removed from the equation. The climatic conditions of the area and the farmers who work the land are also additional factors to be considered.

Sun Yat-sen regarded "distribution of the rights of landownership" as a vital issue. He argued that such rights should not be concentrated in the hands of a few owners but should be given to those who actually work the land. He had the keen foresight to recognize that in the long term landownership by non-tillers would impede productivity.

Soon after I graduated from National Taiwan University in 1947, land reform became a hotly debated issue. I gave a number of speeches advocating the transfer of land to the farmers. My father did not have much land, but he was still a landowner. Naturally, he was opposed to my views. My wife's father, a large landowner, completely disapproved of both my position and my activities.

I responded to both my father and my father-in-law by saying, "It is wrong for people to live well on land rents without working, just because they inherited the property from their ancestors." As a result of the postwar land reform in Taiwan, my father and my relatives lost much of their land assets, which in turn affected my own income as well. Even today, however, I feel I acted correctly, and believe that the land reform was a genuine step forward.

As a specialist in agricultural economics, I have always been concerned about the land problem and have done considerable original research. I applied to study at Iowa State University in 1951 because Theodore W. Schultz taught there. Later a Nobel Prize winner in economics for pioneering research on the importance of human resources in economic development, Schultz was well known for his view that agricultural problems cannot be solved by dealing with agriculture alone. I am in full agreement with this view. In any country, policies on agriculture should be treated together with policies on the nonagricultural sectors.

### Saving Agriculture in Taiwan

At one point I spent about two months in Japan doing research on the "Fundamentals of Agriculture Act" implemented in Japan after World War II. I realized that Taiwan had much to learn from Japan's farm policy. The rural population represented a large majority in the early postwar years, and the Japanese government had adopted various measures to protect agriculture while promoting industrialization. A major turning-point in Japan's agriculture came in the early 1960s. Under the Ikeda Hayato cabinet, the country was experiencing the first years of rapid economic growth. The ever-accelerating tempo of industrialization encroached into farmland and rural areas for factory sites. As a result, farm acreage decreased substantially while land prices rose rapidly.

Similar phenomena occurred in Taiwan during the presidency of Chiang Ching-kuo, except in our case the pace was faster than in Japan. As a minister without portfolio, I was in a position to recommend policies designed to secure the livelihood of farmers, who constituted the overwhelming majority of the population, and at the same time ensure the smooth progress of industrialization. My basic approach was a combination of Sun Yat-sen's idea about "distribution of the rights of landownership" and T. W. Schultz's warning not to isolate agriculture from the nonagricultural sectors.

Formosa Plastics Corporation, one of our fastest-growing corporations, tried to purchase about 4,000 *jia* (approx. 3,880 hectares) of farmland at NT$40,000 per *jia* in one of the counties. Under the law then in force, only farmers were eligible to buy farmland, but the company lobbied the Executive Yuan to revise the law and make corporations eligible as well.

Had the law been changed at that time under pressure from the business community, as much as 100,000 *jia* of farmland all over Taiwan would have been sold to corporations. That would have forced as many as 100,000 farm households out of agriculture. Worse, that would have affected half a million people, assuming an average of five people per farm household.

Given the condition of the state coffers and the socio-economic situation in Taiwan in those days, it would have been impossible to provide jobs or relief funds for half a million people. Allowing corporations to purchase farmland would have created massive unemployment without any way to deal with it.

I could not let this happen. I had to fight to prevent the revision of the law governing transactions in agricultural land. But I was virtually the only one in government who opposed the proposed revision. My only hope was President Chiang Ching-kuo. Somehow I had to persuade him to back me up. I said to President Chiang, "Our industries are not yet sufficiently developed. There is talk of a labor shortage nowadays, but that shortage is exceedingly small when compared with the number of unemployed farmers that will result from farmland acquisition by industries. Rather than allowing them to sell their farmland, we should help the rural areas by injecting capital from the nonagricultural sectors and try to raise the overall productivity of the economy."

Fortunately, President Chiang concurred, and the worst-case scenario was averted. It took some years, however, before the tangible effects of the decision became apparent. Quite recently, I spoke to a caddy at a golf course, who happened to come from the village where Formosa Plastics tried to buy up farmland back in the 1980s, only to be thwarted by my opposition.

"How is everyone in your village?" I asked the caddy. "My father and the villagers are all grateful to you, Mr. President," was his reply. The land price had skyrocketed about a thousand times in the past fifteen years or so, from NT$40,000 per *jia* to a range between NT$30 million and NT$50 million. "The villagers are really glad that they did not sell their land at such a low price," said the caddy. It was gratifying to know that the story of my opposition had been handed down in the villages.

## What Is Taiwan's Identity?

One reason I was valuable to President Chiang Ching-kuo was my expertise in an important area encumbered by many serious problems, which was of course agriculture. Besides, he knew that he did not need to worry about the possibility of my getting involved in any radical revolutionary activities.

Actually he and I had a lot in common, besides the fact that we had both studied Marxism at one time. At the close of several days of interrogating me in 1969, a Taiwan Garrison Command officer said to me, "No one but Chiang Ching-kuo would dare to use someone like you." Apparently, he was referring to my adventurous intellectual background. I must say, I tried to live up to Chiang's faith in me. But when it came to the issue of Taiwan's identity, we had our differences.

President Chiang Ching-kuo did not necessarily choose me as his vice-president with the thought that I would one day succeed him. At that time, with no idea that he would become ill and die so quickly, he wasn't thinking about his successor yet. I remember him telling me once, "I am a Taiwanese," but I don't think he ever thought about what kind of political culture best suited the Taiwanese people.

It is impossible to form a political culture that embodies Taiwan's identity without, first and foremost, an intense love for Taiwan itself. I say this all the time, but the person who will lead Taiwan in the future must be a real fighter, someone who loves Taiwan deeply and will shed blood, sweat, and tears for Taiwan.

That is easy to say, but what is "Taiwan's identity"? Some

might answer right off, "an independent Taiwan." I, for one, do not believe that independence is the only option available to make Taiwan's position in international society completely clear. It is more important for us to establish ourselves as the Republic of China on Taiwan.

In my recommendations for political reform, I cited "Republic of China on Taiwan" as the phrase that best represents the position we are establishing. Under that term, our jurisdiction covers Taiwan, the Pescadores, Quemoy, and Matsu, but not mainland China. As soon as I stated that policy, there was a critical reaction that I was not interested in carrying on a relationship with the Chinese mainland. I believe that before we do anything else, Taiwan has to get its own house firmly in order. If Taiwan's identity is not completely clear to its people, how can we deal with mainland China?

The first step is to convince the international community of our identity and our place in the world. Only then can we think about China as a whole.

### A Model for a Reunified China

Setting priorities does not mean that we are unconcerned about the future of China as a whole. How Taiwan should be involved is not just a critical issue for Taiwan but will have a great deal of significance for mainland China.

Chinese civilization is said to be four thousand years old, and some say five, but whichever it is, that is a vast accumulation of time for the Chinese cultural sphere. On the surface it seems grand, but if you examine that history closely, you will find that it is a sad chronicle of advance and decline recurring again and again. When China is seen in that perspective, it is no wonder that Europeans used to talk about the "stagnation of Asia."

In modern times China certainly tried to pull itself up and out of the stagnant, repetitious cycle of history, first through the Nationalist revolution and then the Communist revolution. We can only wonder with regret what might have been if the Nationalist revolution had not been interrupted on the mainland before it was completed, making way for the Communist revolution. There, too, mainland China was once again caught in the vicious circle of its stagnant history.

What did the Communist revolution accomplish? It did not bring the continent out of stagnation or free the people of stifling, oppressive tradition; what it did do was resurrect "hegemony" and imperialism. Economic production appears to have increased under the "socialist market economy," but the thinking behind it has not changed. Mainland China's economy may be growing, but political reform has not progressed at all.

The situation in the mainland now leads me to believe that Taiwan is the one to provide a model for all China in the future. The August 3, 1998 issue of *The Wall Street Journal* contains an article I wrote entitled "The U.S. Can't Ignore Taiwan," in which I openly suggest that the best model for the social, economic, and political reforms in Chinese society can be found in none other than Taiwan:

In recent times, communist China and some people in the West have accused the Republic of China of carrying on a campaign for "Taiwan independence," "two Chinas," or "one China, one Taiwan." This is a total distortion of the truth.

What we on Taiwan have done all along is preserve, for China, a piece of land that is free from communist rule. We have developed the economy and have embraced democracy, becoming the model for a future reunified China.

Our goal has been to transform the structure of the economy from labor-intensive industry to technology-intensive industry and to steadily reduce the weight of agriculture. Today manufacturing accounts for 35 percent of the gross domestic product, the service sector accounts for 62 percent, and agriculture for 3 percent.

We have also revised the Constitution to provide for election of the president by direct popular vote, and we have made progress in implementing administrative reforms in the government. In education as well as in the judiciary, restructuring and reform are under way, and once they are established, they will constitute the firm foundation for a sustainable democratic society.

As in the past, mainland China is mired in its historical nemesis—the repeated cycle of advance and decline, never moving positively ahead. The causes are, first of all, a system that has entrusted policymaking to a few individual leaders, so that all decisions have been implemented without listening to the voice of the people. Second, without a forward-looking vision, necessary changes in the social structure have been long neglected, and third, the leaders have ignored the need to address the people's welfare. Government policies giving low priority to the citizens have brought uncertainty to social development and hampered progress in the Chinese mainland.

Conversely, the people of Taiwan have pulled themselves and their country out of stagnation and have continued to persevere in their efforts. Why was it possible in Taiwan? I would say it was because of Taiwan's diversity. Just as I continued on my intellectual journey, encountering many different ways of thinking, I grew and changed. Taiwan is growing and changing in the same way, blessed by the many cultures, institutions, and ways of thinking that are at home in Taiwan.

# CHAPTER **2**

# My Political Philosophy

I AM not a politician. True, I have served as minister without portfolio, mayor of the city of Taipei, governor of Taiwan Province, and then as vice-president of the Republic of China before becoming its president. Given this career, it may seem odd to say such a thing. Nevertheless, I do not consider myself a politician for several reasons.

If you look at what government has meant in Chinese history you will understand my reluctance to be called a politician. It has meant ruling people, and nothing else. In China's cultural tradition, politicians have been members of the elite who hold power over people. Although the old style of politics is still practiced on the mainland, I am proud to say that "government" in the traditional sense is a thing of the past in Taiwan. If a politician is someone who controls people, the term does not apply to me.

Another reason I do not consider myself a politician is that I do not make political deals in order to win my objectives. What I have done, rather, is to work on many programs designed to develop Taiwan into a modern, industrial democracy. It has been my duty and challenge to think of what needed to be done for the sake of Taiwan and to carry it out. Government does require one to engage in sometimes fierce bargaining and confrontation on every front, but I do not believe that Taiwan needs such political struggle now. I may be an administrator, but I am definitely not a political wheeler-dealer.

The slogan I adopted when I took office as seventh-term President of the ROC in January 1988 upon the death of my predecessor, Chiang Ching-kuo, was "One Mind and Purpose, Unify as

One." All I could say as a new national leader with little background in so-called politics was, "Let us work together for this country."

During my election campaign for the eighth-term presidency, I called for the building of a new era for the Chinese people. I presented a set of specific programs, but my focus was on the Chinese people as a whole, not on Taiwan or the nation. In 1996, when I was inaugurated as ninth-term president, I began to stress Taiwan, declaring that "We have entered an era when sovereignty resides in the people." Earlier, during the election campaign, I spoke of the necessity to listen to the voices of the people and to undertake thoroughgoing democratic reforms. Then I called for the creation of a new center of culture founded on "Great Taiwan." I also expressed to voters my firm resolve to serve the people from beginning to end. If I call myself a politician, it is only insofar as the term denotes a person who listens to what people have to say and does his best to put into practice what they demand of government.

## Two Types of Nationalism
I first stressed Taiwan in my acceptance speech for the nomination as KMT presidential candidate in August 1995. In that speech I voiced my conviction that Taiwan can fully express its free will and build a bright future only when there is popular sovereignty. I said:

> As leader of this country, I have upheld the ideal of popular sovereignty. This is also the principle advocated by Nationalist

revolutionary leader, Dr. Sun Yat-sen. The people of our society already have a strong awareness of popular sovereignty today. We all possess the aspiration to be masters of this state. However, we have not yet fully understood the meaning of "symbiotic community." We have just begun to practice democratic government, and our institutionalization process has not caught up with democratic development. Therefore, we must admit that different opinions exist in this society, which affect the formation of a symbiotic community. This goal can only be achieved through our mutual understanding, cooperation, wisdom, tolerance, and brotherly love.

Then I added as follows:

As you know, Taiwan is a society of immigrants. Most of its population, except the indigenous people who were here from ancient times, came from the continent. Whether early settlers or late arrivals, all of us cultivated this land by the sweat of our brows, throwing ourselves heart and soul into making Taiwan what it is today. It is meaningless and unnecessary to argue over who is Taiwanese and who is not, merely following the yardstick of who came when. Believing that Taiwan is ours, loving Taiwan and wholeheartedly devoting ourselves to its cause—these are the real significances of being Taiwanese. We should promote this vision of "new Taiwanese." We are also Chinese so long as we respect the legacy of Chinese culture and not forget the ideal of China's reunification.

Analyzing this inauguration speech, a political scientist concluded that it reflects two types of nationalism in Taiwan, one focused on the Taiwanese territorial concept of Great Taiwan, and the other a cultural nationalism centering on Chinese culture.

## New Center of Chinese Culture

The issue here is not which of the two types of nationalism is more legitimate. Rather, it is a question of how to establish a solid Taiwanese identity. What I emphasized in my 1995 speech was "management" of Great Taiwan and the building of a new center of Chinese culture. Let me cite part of the speech here:

> Amid the rich influence of many different cultures over a long period of time, and the overall progress of Chinese civilization, Taiwan is becoming an advanced new force and a new center of Chinese culture. This is a golden opportunity for us to leave behind the trials of history and for all different groups to harmoniously unite together to open up a new era for managing Great Taiwan and establishing a new center of Chinese culture.

A "new center" is essentially a place where culture mixes and flourishes. Put in more political terms, it is the prospering of democratic culture. Democratic culture can be acquired only when all people living in Taiwan are involved in its nurture. A national identity—that "we are Taiwanese"—will be born out of that participation and provide the basis for a democratic culture in Taiwan.

It will be impossible to establish such an identity if dividing lines are drawn separating the offspring of early settlers from the continent, those who moved to Taiwan with the Kuomintang and their offspring, and those descended from the indigenous people. To realize the potential of Great Taiwan, it is crucial that all people of different historical backgrounds come together, forming a new common background distinct from that of the continent. To that end, what lawmakers in Taiwan should do for the people is: first, manage Great Taiwan in a democratic and efficient way; second, promote industrial development and scientific advancement; and third, create an environment in which people can enjoy comfortable and secure family lives. These three policies, that is, political, industrial, and social policies, should form the basis for making steady progress in reforms in the government, the judiciary, and in education.

### Qualifications of Taiwanese Politicians

What is required of Taiwan's politicians in order to carry out these reforms? An essential condition of a future president of Taiwan is that he or she should love Taiwan and be devoted to its people, as I said earlier. If a person fulfills these conditions, what image of him or her as a political leader will emerge when viewed in the context of the "new center" of culture that Taiwan aspires to?

To explain this, let me again evoke Sun Yat-sen's "the world is for all" motto. This means that government should not be run for a specific group of people and that politicians should be unselfish. By "unselfish" is meant that in his or her actions and deeds, a politician should put aside personal interest. In making a decision, a politician should think of the best course of action others might have chosen had he or she not been there.

Thinking along these lines, a political leader will be able to remain level-headed and focus on the genuine good of the nation. Conscious of your duty as a policy maker, you can make decisions that put the interests of society above that of individuals.

Of course, this is easier said than done. It is extremely difficult to practice completely selfless service to the people. Human beings have such strong tendencies toward self-centeredness that even a person of the noblest character finds it hard to put his or her own desires aside when considering matters of public concern.

Making sure that the people receive sincere consideration is a great challenge, but it is not the only duty a politician must fulfill. Merely considering the welfare of the people is not good enough. The more essential objective of a lawmaker should be to pave the way for realizing objectives that people cannot achieve by themselves.

The "world is for all" idea can be said to be exactly the same as the Christian idea of love I arrived at after a long spiritual journey. By placing ourselves in the position of others and endeavoring to provide what they seek, we can achieve virtue that is close to the love of God described in the Bible.

I often quote from the Bible. The thirteenth chapter in the "Epistles of Paul the Apostle to the Corinthians" has a passage on love, which I frequently cite:

Love is kind and patient,
never jealous, boastful,
proud, or rude.

Love isn't selfish
or quick-tempered.
It doesn't keep a record
of wrongs that others do.
Love rejoices in the truth,
but not in evil.
Love is always supportive,
loyal, hopeful,
and trusting.
Love never fails!
(I Corinthians, 13: 4-7)

Striving to put oneself in "the other man's shoes" when thinking about things, and working to achieve objectives without seeking personal gain is the essence of "love," and that is what
"government" is all about for me.

## Taking the Roundabout Course

Love is "patient . . . and trusting," as taught in the Bible. In my
personal experience in the world of politics as well, patience is
extremely important. Politics often demands immediate results,
so the choices politicians make tend to reflect that behest. Under
the democratic system, people judge politicians by their achievements; it is only natural that politicians are eager to get results
that people will instantly recognize. All too often, of course, such
choices turn out to be the wrong ones, leading their country down
the wrong road.

In confronting problems, politicians should be careful not to
jump too quickly and simplistically to conclusions. They must

not just take the shortest path to their objective. Instead of attempting to find a way that leads directly to their destination, they should examine the merits of a more roundabout approach. The value of avoiding excessively blunt or strong-arm tactics, in favor of more flexible, indirect approaches, can be found not only in politics but in dealing with economic and social issues as well. The former often ends up taking more time, ultimately failing to achieve the objective after all.

This is what often happens, for example, when you are trying to reach a destination by car. You may think that it is bothersome to circle around the ramp and go through the tollbooth to get on the turnpike, when the path to your destination seems to stretch in a straight line before you by the regular road. But then you may find yourself caught in a traffic jam and end up taking far longer anyway. Even though the turnpike may seem to be the roundabout route, it will enable you to reach your destination several times faster. There are numerous cases in the realm of politics where what I call the "turnpike theory" can be fittingly applied. The greater your objective, moreover, the more useful you will find the roundabout strategy and the more important it is to refrain from thinking about what may seem the quicker, more direct solution.

An easy and immediately effective way to achieve economic growth, for example, is to introduce a large amount of foreign capital and invite foreign corporations for offshore production. By bringing in foreign capital and enterprises, a country can achieve economic growth within a short span of time. This direct method, however, can easily exhaust a country, as demonstrated by the economic crisis of Asia that started with the plunge in value of the Thai baht in July 1997.

The greater the scale of your objective, the more necessary it is to consider the indirect way. Economic growth based mainly on financial transactions, for example, cannot be sustained for long, and it does not genuinely benefit people. An industrial development policy, moreover, cannot lay the foundation for industry if it destroys agriculture.

Agricultural productivity must be increased in the long term. Development of industry and acquisition of advanced technology should be based on that premise, and the accumulation of capital thereby paves the way for creating a sound financial base. Efforts such as this will lead to real development.

## Politics to Win Votes Is Harmful to the Country

Let me cite some specific cases to illustrate these points from our experience in Taiwan. The issue of agricultural reform in Taiwan is an excellent example of where the "roundabout" approach ought to be applied.

Suppose your task is to increase land productivity to support economic growth. If you think you have to complete the task immediately, you have only to invest capital in the farmland where productivity is low. You may ease regulations on the purchase and sale of agricultural land so that not only owner-farmers but also individuals and corporations can buy and sell farmland freely. This allows corporations to enter the agricultural industry and undertake cost-effective farm management, thereby increasing land productivity. The reasoning here seems to be sound. To farmers, too, there does not seem to be anything wrong with selling their farmland if they can obtain a fair price; they are already in the process of becoming part-time farmers in any case.

If the market for farmland were liberalized without any regulation, farmland would almost certainly become the target of speculation. It would not necessarily be used for farming. The price of some land would surge and be diverted to industrial and residential purposes. The result would be the proliferation of jobless ex-farmers who have given up their land.

The ill-considered liberalization of the farmland market would, therefore, lead to lower productivity in Taiwan, so some regulation is clearly necessary. At the same time, the social and industrial structure centered around agriculture cannot be maintained forever. The farming population will eventually decrease; if it does not, indeed, there would be little hope for Taiwan's development.

This is the reason that, as governor of Taiwan Province, I sought to prevent drastic liberalization and at the same time energize "core farming households" which could be counted on to run highly productive farm operations in the future. I argued that it was possible to conceive a future vision of Taiwanese agriculture by creating 80,000 core farming households and having their children learn the latest farming technologies in agricultural school. Today the second generation of these core farming households are working hard to raise agricultural productivity even further. By the time these young people become the backbone of the nation's agriculture, they can set up agricultural corporations and operate farming on a large scale. There will be little worry that this might lead to putting many people out of work because Taiwan has already become an industrial nation equipped with the latest technology and industry and because its farming population has been substantially reduced.

If this roundabout policy had not been taken and the purchase and sale of farmland fully liberalized, Taiwan would not be what it is today. In politics or the economy, we should never forget the validity of the turnpike theory. The more democratized a nation becomes, the more essential roundabout policies will be, for in a democracy the votes a politician can win depends to a large extent upon the policies he or she advocates.

Some skeptics declare that "this kind of policy may be necessary in long-term perspective, but you can't get votes that way." Such concerns may prove valid, but it can be prevented if politicians are free to engage in fair debates on policy before the public. If it can be cogently demonstrated through the mass media that such-and-such a policy may not have an immediate effect but is still necessary for Taiwan's future, long-term policies will win popular support. If everyone continues to pursue immediate gains, of course, no progress will be made.

## Does Democracy Really "Spoil" People?

Some may call me to task for thinking that it is possible to trust the people's judgment and convince them of the value of long-term, often roundabout policies through public discussion and debate. People who become accustomed to the permissiveness of a democratic system, they say, will certainly prefer immediate gain. I do not deny that possibility. A look at history clearly shows that democracy has its negative side. The argument that democracy "spoils" the people is difficult to accept in total, but in a society that has become democratized over a short period of time, there is a real danger that politics will be conducted with little more purpose than to please the masses.

To solve that problem, there is no choice but to leave the matter up to time. Democracy itself is a roundabout approach; it differs from dictatorship, which seeks to fulfill political objectives directly and impatiently. The maturity of a democracy is best attained in a roundabout manner.

For that reason I do not agree that a combination of the free market and democracy means the end of history as portrayed by Francis Fukuyama in *The End of History and the Last Man*, (1993). One cannot say that the attainment of liberal democracy is some kind of ultimate destination.

Even the United States, which has advocated the cause of liberal democracy since its founding as a nation, struggles with many internal problems. The gap between rich and poor is becoming wider, for example. The forces of capitalism are so strong in the United States that there is the danger that business may control politics. The problems of ethnic minorities also remain unresolved.

Liberal democracy is not a system capable of speedily solving problems. No matter how stridently people demand immediate improvement of specific conditions, meaningful progress can be made only in a roundabout way. A direct and forceful approach to improvement is bound to produce friction and distortion. Likewise, liberal democracy in Taiwan in no way represents the "end of history"; on the contrary, it has just begun. We must solve the many problems confronting us slowly and steadily, and we must not be afraid to take the long way around to get there.

**Tectonic Movement in Liberal Democracy**

Let us consider a little further the situation of liberal democratic nations today, including the United States. In *The Future of Capitalism: How Today's Economic Forces Shape Tomorrow's World* (1996), MIT professor Lester C. Thurow explains the challenges confronting the world in terms of the simultaneous movements of five economic "tectonic plates." First, communism ended in the Soviet Union and Eastern Europe, greatly changing the complexion of the political world map. The change also led to the rapid expansion of market capitalism.

Second, brainpower industries surged to the fore through rapid advances in information and communications technology. This trend has wrought many changes in the structure of political and economic institutions. Third, the world's population has increased by explosive proportions, and demographic movement is vigorous. The population of industrialized nations, furthermore, is rapidly aging. Fourth, the economy is globalizing at a fierce pace, complicating and destabilizing the relationships between the market and the state and between economics and politics. Fifth, since the collapse of the Soviet Union, the United States has become the world's only superpower, but its unipolar dominance is eroding.

These five radical changes Thurow discusses are closely related to one another. The expansion of market capitalism, the information and computer revolution, the movement of people, globalization, and the change in U.S. dominance are all simply different facets of the same overall whirlpool of change.

Any country in the world that attempts to operate as a liberal democracy inevitably enters this whirlpool. Capitalism's huge, computerized market will be a pivotal force for the development of democracy. At the same time, in the suddenly globally linked world, the speed and volume of capital and demographic movement are sometimes so intense that social security systems and the labor supply are destabilized.

Themselves caught up in this furious current, today's politicians are finding it increasingly difficult to identify solid criteria upon which to formulate policies. And with change occurring at such a rapid pace, it is difficult for them to judge the proper timing for implementation of the policies they do formulate.

This is not the first time that liberal democracy—economically hinging on the free market and politically reliant on democratic government—has confronted enormous challenges. Communism, which surged into power in Russia during World War I, rejected the free market and democracy, advocating in their place the planned economy and dictatorship of the proletariat. In the wake of the confusion following World War I, fascist and Nazi dictatorships emerged from controlled economies and demagoguery. These regimes, too, represented a rejection of liberal democracy.

Have these challenges—from forces of communism and fascism that have virtually disappeared—been overcome? In fact, they have not. As long as the free market economy exercises destructive power and democracy is vulnerable to political malfunction, such reactionary ideologies will remain a threat to liberal democracy.

The threat of communism and fascism to liberal democracy is visible and their arguments are clear and easy to grasp. By contrast, the tectonic movements described by Thurow are much greater in scale and may be far more difficult to deal with as they perpetrate confrontation between capitalism and democracy.

Thurow argues that democracy and capitalism differ radically in the distribution of power. As he puts it, "Democracy believes in 'one man, one vote' (equality of political power), while capitalism believes in letting the market rule (in practice, great inequalities in economic power)." The survival-of-the-fittest principle and inequalities in purchasing power, Thurow maintains, form the basis of capitalism.

Some call Thurow's arguments extreme, yet the potential conflict between capitalism and democracy he addresses has some validity, and as globalization progresses there is the danger that the problem may be further aggravated. Political leaders must think about these tremendously complex and difficult circumstances and plan for the future of their countries. Taiwan is no exception.

## Taiwan amid the Tectonic Shifts

Taiwan is now endeavoring, while heeding the voices of the people, to create a society in which citizens can freely pursue their activities. This can only be achieved through the rule of law. In order to promote free competition, there must be rules for the game. Without regulation of any kind, competition is bound to be excessive.

Taiwan's challenge was that it had to simultaneously carry out, in only a few decades, what the United States, Japan, and other industrially advanced nations had already achieved over a much longer period. In May 1948, a year after the February 28 Incident, the Temporary Provisions Effective During the Period of National Mobilization for Suppression of the Communist Rebellion (hereafter referred to as "Temporary Provisions") was promulgated, and martial law was proclaimed in May the following year. Until martial law was abolished in July 1987 and the Temporary Provisions rescinded in May 1991, Taiwan was in a prolonged state of national emergency.

In addition to the peculiar circumstances of its own history and political geography, Taiwan is confronted with many problems that plague even the United States and other major industrial nations. For example, the greater the progress Taiwan makes in democratization, the greater its responsibilities become with regard to social security. A national medical care insurance system was launched in 1995, and today 96 percent of the people of Taiwan are subscribers. Before the system's adoption, few households could afford to take their children or elderly members to the doctor because medical fees were so high. Today, anyone can receive adequate medical treatment. Learning from the experience of the industrial countries, we determined that it is not necessary to adopt a medical insurance system comparable to the high level introduced by Sweden. Instead, we found a system that is feasible and appropriate for today's Taiwan.

When indigenous Taiwanese become unemployed, for example, they should not be left to fend for themselves because they can no longer afford to pay insurance premiums. There has to be a way for the government to tide them over temporarily.

Furthermore, even corporations that have been run well and profitably may at some point go into decline, sometimes suddenly closing down without paying employees for severance or retirement. Employees who are unilaterally laid off immediately face difficulties in maintaining their livelihood. There needs to be a system to cope with such contingencies.

We should recall that welfare was among Sun Yat-sen's Three Principles of the People. I tell the people that our Nationalist Party is able to deal satisfactorily with problems such as those mentioned above. I have repeatedly said, "The most important task for the government is to understand fully and tackle the problems faced by the country. People with problems should come directly to the government to tell us what they require or even stage a demonstration if they feel it necessary."

### The Civil Minimum Tested in Taipei

My experience as mayor of the city of Taipei starting in 1978 was instrumental in shaping my commitment to the principle of listening to what people have to say so as to make government better. While I was mayor I studied in detail the principles of city management. I read various books, including a series on urban problems published by Iwanami Shoten in Tokyo, and examined the subject from many different angles. I also conducted detailed surveys of specific problems. Together with city assembly members, I frequently attended community meetings to hear about various social problems and complaints. I brought these back to city hall and discussed them with officials from the responsible sections of the municipal government. I was able to obtain cooperation from city assembly members because I had compiled a database about each of them and knew their experience and character well. Some of them complained that the database was based on "secret investigations." Actually, the data included, for example, whether the person liked to drink, and how much he or she could drink. Needless to say, the database also contained information about the support base each assembly member relied on at election time.

During my three-and-a-half-year term as mayor I became so familiar with the city that I knew what road or street had which particular problems, and which areas had poor sewerage systems. I inspected almost every street on foot, and even went down the sewers to observe their condition firsthand. On the basis of those observations, I realized that if the sewers were cleaned by February or March at the latest, before the arrival of the typhoon season, many street problems could be solved. In Taiwan today, Taipei is the only city that is free of garbage disposal problems, the reason being that many incinerators were built while I was mayor.

I discovered that the crux of urban planning is to gather solid data. Per capita income, average standard of living, size of domicile, and other such data have to be accurate; otherwise it is virtually impossible to plan where bus stations should be built, what problems have to be dealt with concerning gas utility facilities, how many more schools are needed, and so forth.

I found the know-how of urban planning in Japan to be very useful. Precedents in the United States, where the environment is vastly different from that in Taiwan, were of less help. I used the example of Osaka as my basic model. In reporting to the municipal assembly I presented my city planning schemes by assigning "civil-minimum indexes" to them. This was the first attempt at utilizing the civil minimum in Taiwan. Civil-minimum indexes represent the welfare levels to be achieved, using symbols such as the mathematical sign sigma. They clearly indicate the predictable effects of electing specific priorities. In short, the indexes readily show the levels of welfare attained in an area after the allocation of a certain amount of tax revenues to that particular area.

The assembly reacted to the use of civil-minimum indexes favorably, enabling us to discuss city planning in detail by means of the indexes. When the gap between the figures and reality seemed to be too great, we adjusted the budget allocation as well as the order of priorities and deliberated until all were persuaded. This way of doing things not only helped convince the assembly but also contributed to a better understanding of the city administration among citizens.

## Evaluation of Idealism in U.S. Politics

In addition to local administrative issues, Taiwan has also formulated many policies in the areas of financial and information industries in order to deal with the drastically changing international environment. The people of Taiwan must work together in coping with the problems that accompany the shifting of Thurow's economic tectonic plates. Specific measures will be discussed in the following chapters, but here let us take a further look at the United States, a country that has had enormous influence on my political philosophy.

For Taiwan, the United States is our best guide in facilitating economic development and promoting democracy. Partly because it is a society of immigrants, like Taiwan, I found the United States easy to live in and open even to a person like me from a foreign country. A young person completely unknown and without connections can achieve great success there in a short space of time, which is certainly one of the reasons it continues to attract people from all over the world.

Taiwan has similar features. It, too, is an immigrant society, a melting pot of several ethnic groups and cultures. There are also opportunities for an ordinary person to rise quickly and achieve great success. If you start a venture business and fail, no one will reproach you. Taiwan is very different in this respect from Japan, where an entrepreneur whose company goes bankrupt loses the confidence of society and his status therein. Taiwan should therefore learn more from American society. We need to study how to maintain the liberal and open dimensions of society and how to foster the dynamic energies of our people.

World political affairs cannot be fully understood without due attention to the development of U.S. politics, and in that sense, too, we become inveterate observers of movements in Washington. Henry Kissinger says, in his book *Diplomacy* (1996), that balance-of-power relations with other countries influence U.S. foreign policy. As I see it, however, American foreign policy is continually swinging from side to side like a pendulum, making it difficult to understand. This is caused by the dynamics of American politics arising from the tensions between the administration and Congress. When the president decides to adopt a certain policy, the Congress may assert totally different alternatives, which even the president cannot ignore.

Take the United States' current policy on mainland China, for example. Eager to achieve immediate results, the administration has a strong tendency to deal with problems in a technical manner. The Congress, on the other hand, which remains the bastion of American idealism, tends to insist on the importance of democracy, freedom, and human rights. That is why U.S. China policy often gives an impression that it is rife with contradictions, swinging back and forth between two extremes.

Even so, it is idealism that forms the core of U.S. politics. It often happens that the president pushes through his policies, but idealism reasserts itself soon afterward, causing a movement to restrain purely realist measures on the part of the administration. I admire this American idealism, because it is indispensable in an immigrant society that harbors within it many complex contradictions. In managing a country of ethnic diversity where cultural friction is a way of life, idealism that rises above such

*My Political Philosophy* ▊ 79

friction is absolutely necessary. In that sense as well, American politics is a good model for Taiwan.

### Political Caliber of Japan

Japan has been a valuable teacher. Not only in the area of urban issues, mentioned earlier, but also in dealing with agricultural problems and the fostering of industry, Taiwan learned a great deal from it.

After the Plaza Accord reached by the Group of Five industrialized nations in 1985, there were quite a number of cases in which Japan looked as if it did not know what it was doing. Most notably, its decisions vis-à-vis economic issues have sometimes been so awkward that they provoked international criticism. What is most responsible for this situation seems to be the passing down of political leadership to family members in Japan, a tendency that is rarely seen in the United States and Taiwan.

This hereditary tendency is often mentioned in the context of Japanese social issues, but in my opinion its effects are more dangerous in the world of politics. Now it is almost impossible for a young person to climb up from complete obscurity and gain election to the Diet. A fairly large number of Diet members today are the children or grandchildren of former Diet members.

Until some time after the end of World War II, there was room for even a "nobody" to succeed in Japan's political world, and this was a source of vitality in its society. In politics, business, and other fields, the remarkable rise of postwar Japan was attributable to such newcomers from obscure backgrounds.

Going back further to the Meiji era (1868–1912), as pointed out by the late novelist Shiba Ryotaro, the change of leaders in various fields was so drastic and sweeping that it looked as if a brand-new Japan had been born under the Meiji state.

I still read more books from Japan than from any other country. It has a rich accumulation of scholarship and research in science, technology, and other areas. In the future, an important challenge for Japan will be to display this depth in the field of politics. I will discuss this further in the third and fifth chapters.

# CHAPTER **3**

# The Dynamics of
# Peace and Prosperity

THE ECONOMIC development of Japan has taught Taiwan a great deal. Our industrialization got its start, literally, with the factories, roads, and other infrastructure the Japanese had built before and during World War II and by utilizing the accumulated economic resources of management know-how and technology remaining there at the end of the war.

It was not until the takeoff of economic development and industrialization that local Taiwanese elements came into play. Only today has Taiwan become concerned with the originality of its industry. The major challenge now is how to achieve technological and organizational transformation. As the transformation takes place, quality rather than quantity will be what really matters, and original Taiwanese approaches will be crucial.

Today the Japanese economy is weighed down by many problems, and in the absence of effective policy measures, the impact of its prolonged recession is beginning to be felt in neighboring countries as well. In my view, however, Japan possesses great potential but does not seem to be able to utilize it to best advantage.

One aspect of Japan's industrialization that has been particularly useful for Taiwan is its careful research in technological development. Sufficient study of which industries should be promoted, and in what directions, can help prevent major distortions in the industrial structure that could impede economic development. Postwar Japan very cleverly avoided this pitfall. Taiwan, too, has been careful to consider the proper direction for its technological development.

We also learned much from Japan in the area of industrial

and corporate organization. After the war, Japan made no attempt to set up huge integrated organizations such as those that existed in the United States, forming instead core organizations surrounded by "satellite" bodies. This "core-satellite" style of organization allowed for flexible responses to market changes. It also adapted well in developing practices for the improvement of quality.

Whereas in Japan the core-satellite organization consisted of the parent company's relatively large plant and small subsidiary factories, in Taiwan there were many cases in which smaller-scale factories joined hands. This feature developed from small-scale farm management that was characteristic of both Taiwanese and Japanese tradition.

## Promotion of Small and Medium-scale Corporations

Taiwan has also adopted the small-group activity formula that Japanese management has successfully used to enhance solidarity among employees in the workplace. Group members come to the office early in the morning to clean and tidy up, for example, hold morning assemblies before starting to work, and enjoy various forms of recreation together.

As a student in Japan at Kyoto Imperial University, I studied business management first and then learned about small-farm management. "Business management" in those days meant American-style systems such as those developed by Frederick Taylor and Henry Ford. Essentially, they consisted of a huge pyramidal organization and very specific divisions of labor. This method is ideal for mass production, but it is not flexible because everything needed is produced in the factory itself. The compartmentalization of the enterprise inhibits the flow of information within the plant and makes it difficult for the organization to respond to rapid changes in the market. A bigger problem with the system is the difficulty of effective financial risk management. Because the enterprise is responsible for everything it needs, the system is fine as long as each part works smoothly, but should something go wrong, trouble tends to accumulate, leading to heavy losses.

Japanese-style organization, on the other hand, is such that parts are produced at different subcontractor factories and supplied as needed. This does not involve much risk for the core factory, where the parts are assembled according to market demand. This is the strongest point of Japanese-style management.

Building on this organizational formula, Japan achieved remarkable growth in the manufacturing sector. U.S. industry, burdened by mammoth-scale organizations that were difficult to scale down, suffered greatly in the 1970s and 1980s.

By adopting the Japanese-style organizational concept in manufacturing, Taiwan was able to achieve rapid economic growth. Through the core-satellite organization, we have managed to build an efficient, low-risk industrial structure.

### The Shift in Industrial Structure
Taiwan's economic policy is currently pursuing the gradual privatization of state enterprises. All state enterprises will be placed under private management on a predetermined schedule. For example, although the government-run electric power

corporation has not been privatized yet, the private sector has already been allowed to invest in the electric power business. I have urged the electric power corporation to solicit private investment if they have facilities and land that are idle.

In the telecommunications business, the government's Directorate General of Telecommunications, which initially handled this industry, has now been partially reorganized into the China Telecommunications Corporation. Thus, the first stage of privatization has begun in this area, too. As for banks, several have been operated by the government, but all will come under private management.

Partly because I myself initiated and promoted various farming and other industrial policies, I am often prompted to think about how things could be further improved in one sector or how developments in another might offer the promise of new business opportunities. As president of the Republic of China on Taiwan, however, I and other government officials must refrain from intruding in the specifics of private sector activity. Too much interference from above could hinder the sound progress of industry.

The greatest impediments to Taiwan corporations in their endeavors to enter new fields of business are the scarcity of land and capital, as well as lack of the supplementary technology. Solving such basic problems still requires vigorous government assistance.

Japan did well in sensitively handling these interlinked processes of industrialization, and Taiwan has much to learn from its experience. Especially at a time when our economy has advanced to the stage of industrial transformation and upgrading, the experiences of postwar Japan will be all the more valuable.

## Taiwan-specific Development and Issues

While learning a great deal from Japan, Taiwan has not necessarily moved along the same path of development. Taiwan naturally has problems peculiar to it that must be resolved by specifically Taiwanese approaches.

One consideration, stemming perhaps from the traits of its people, is the extremely rapid response of workers to their working conditions. If they find conditions in a workplace intolerable, they promptly move on. The same may be said of investment; if investors decide that a certain investment does not appear to be making a profit, they are quick to shift their funds elsewhere.

Under these circumstances, both corporations and the government have struggled to improve worker training programs. Employees have traditionally not been so quick to change jobs in Japan, although recently this situation seems to have altered somewhat. Japanese workers are more likely to put up with difficult conditions, preferring to stay in one place and acquire certain technical skills.

In Taiwan, by contrast, where workers tend to react quickly to their circumstances, it has been difficult to increase the ranks of skilled workers. They are also very sensitive about their wages in comparison with what others in the same sector are getting. To lower the rate of labor turnover, the government has had to work in various ways to support worker training and education.

Also with regard to employment, the custom of what is known in Japan as lifetime employment has not taken root in Taiwan. In a milieu in which both workers and employers tend to be short-sighted, lifetime employment—employment of workers over an extended period of time—is almost impossible.

Partly because there is relatively little long-term capital investment, Taiwan has no large-scale conglomerates like Japan's Mitsui or Mitsubishi. Even today, 32 percent of Taiwan's gross domestic product is generated by small- and medium-sized enterprises. There are large corporate groups, but they do not match the scale of the major Japanese industrial and financial combines.

Corporate groups in Taiwan have been built mainly through diversification and subsidiary relationships, but they are not structured in such a way that the core company controls the rest of the network. Formosa Plastics Corporation, for example, has grown very large, but in scale and dominance it does not come near Japan's corporate groupings centered around financial institutions.

The industrial policies adopted by the government have had a great deal to do with the loose character of corporate organizations in Taiwan. It did not allow the formation of large conglomerates controlled by core enterprises like Hyundai and Samsung in the Republic of Korea.

Immediately after the end of World War II, basic industries such as steel and shipbuilding that had begun with plant and equipment remaining from the days when Japan controlled the island were operated at first by the government. Private enterprises were left to flourish freely on their own initiatives.

This kind of industrial organization has enhanced the liberal tradition of enterprises in Taiwan, nurturing the conditions for a flexibility that allowed entrepreneurs to take up the challenges that came along. These features of industry will serve Taiwan well in responding to the dramatic changes taking place in the world economy.

## Gradualism in Government

It was only natural that demands for democratization would increase as Taiwan's economy entered its period of rapid growth. The dilemma for the government was how to deal with many intertwined factors. While the people demanded political democratization, a number of problems remained. Would the process of democratization cause economic and social instability, thereby adversely affecting the people's well-being? Had the system of laws changed enough to sustain a democratic state? Was education well enough established to promote the principles and practice of democracy?

Because democratization in Taiwan had to take place amid drastically changing economic conditions, it was by necessity bound up with these sorts of complex problems. To attempt to democratize the political framework without substantive changes in the systems and practices would have made for a frail system indeed.

One of the tasks I faced after being elected as the eighth-term president in 1990 was the rescinding of the Temporary Provisions. This had been instituted to give the government dictatorial powers to mobilize the people in order to deal with the military threat of the Chinese Communist Party.

The Nationalist Party originally enacted the Constitution in 1947, but when the political situation grew tense, the charter was suspended under the said provisions, and the membership of the parliament became permanently fixed. Absolute power was concentrated in the person of the president through the National Security Council, circumventing the Executive Yuan, which is the equivalent of the cabinet.

Even in attempting to abolish the Temporary Provisions, however, the problem was "who" or "what" should abolish it. The provisions had been adopted by the National Assembly; therefore, the solution should have been to re-convene a National Assembly. Yet, at the time, the National Assembly was none other than the "permanent" parliament.

In the first national elections held in China in 1947, representatives had been elected for 2,961 of the total 3,045 seats in the assembly for a term of six years. However, elections were not held again, making those who had been chosen in the first election essentially permanent members of the assembly. To ask the members of the National Assembly to vote to abolish the Temporary Provisions would be tantamount to requiring them to dismiss themselves from office. It was like asking them to dig their own graves or, in any case, pave the road to that end.

No matter how you looked at the problem, it seemed to be an impossible task to persuade them to do such a thing. Yet, without achieving that "impossible task," Taiwan would never see the end of authoritarian government.

What had to be done, I could see, was first to rescind the Temporary Provisions, thereby abolishing the "permanent" parliament. The next step would be to elect representatives to a new National Assembly and Legislative Yuan, bringing together Taiwan's true representatives of the people. Then the Constitution would have to be revised by these representatives in order to bring about democratization. Here again, however, the fundamental problem was how to terminate the formal state of emergency mobilization.

Ultimately, what I did was to visit members of the National Assembly, one at a time. I asked them to retire from their seats and offered them compensation in return. I asked them to retire for the sake of the Republic of China, reminding them of how times had changed and how necessary democratic reforms were for the country. I personally met more than six hundred members.

Even now, I admire the former National Assembly members for accepting my request. They were generous enough to listen to my arguments. Ironical as it was, they were the ones who had elected me president, and yet I had the unenviable task of asking them to retire voluntarily from their positions.

### Demand for Democratization and the Reality Gap
My earnest efforts, however, paid off. In April 1991, a bill for the revision of the Constitution was passed in the National Assembly and in May we were able to proclaim the end of the period of "emergency" and the abolition of the Temporary Provisions. It is necessary to follow democratic procedures in order to achieve progress toward democratization, but inevitably the frictions that

emerge in the process are blamed on the government. There have been charges that "the government talks of democratization, but does little about it," and "the government says it is promoting democratization but adopts only perfunctory measures," and so on. But when you are in a position of democratic leadership you cannot just forcefully do away with your opponents or summarily cut off all those with vested interests in political and economic power. In such a period of transition, government needs time. Time is one of government's greatest resources, and it is important to be able to bide one's time.

From the viewpoint of people demanding democratization in a time of great social change, problems seem to be solvable if one but changes all the institutions that produce them. Any proposal government leaders might proffer appears inadequate. Drastic changes of institutions and laws can nevertheless cause serious social upheaval and chaos.

No matter how literally one might achieve democratization in accordance with popular demand, there will always be discontent and dissatisfaction with the results. There will be those who declare that "It wasn't supposed to turn out this way; the government didn't accomplish real reforms."

While I know that this kind of perception gap is probably inevitable, there is nothing to do but to grapple with each problem, one at a time. We must listen carefully, with empathy and with concern, to the voices of dissatisfaction. It is important to present concrete proposals to address the needs of change. I believe that the perception gap among different political groups can eventually be overcome, through the gradual accumulation of such efforts.

We must wait for the time to be ripe and we must call on the people for support. The kind of political leadership needed is that which attunes itself to the voices of the people in the pursuit of reform and change. The essential work of the politician is to persist in this endeavor. Democratization does not end with the alteration of institutions; what really matters is the patient and committed response to what happens *after that*.

In times like this, government leaders must rid themselves of the authoritarian habits of the past. They must take each and every issue to the people; a political leader will not succeed if he or she does not appeal to popular wisdom and support in search of solutions. Democracy is not possible in Taiwan without politicians who are willing to take the issues to the people.

## "Existence" Is the Key

As important as democratization, and in fact closely connected with that process, is the issue of foreign relations. Should we fail to steer a steady course for Taiwan's foreign policy, not only the success of democratization but its very survival will be endangered. For a long time, I have managed to maintain the delicate balance of the Republic of China's diplomacy, and I am often asked to explain my "secret." In fact, it is extremely plain and simple. It is only to hold firmly to the principle that Taiwan exists. Taiwan's existence is a fact, and as long as Taiwan exists, there is hope. For any democratization or economic development to come about, Taiwan must first *exist*.

What do we do to make certain that Taiwan exists? First we need relations with other countries. Formal diplomatic relations are, of course, the best, but when that is impossible, practical relations centering on economic ties are effective as well. Should even economic links be difficult, then cultural ties should be pursued. There are many ways of cultivating relations with other countries that do not involve embassies. Similarly, there is no reason for not cultivating ties with other countries just because there are no official channels. The strengthening of private ties with people of other countries, including the maintenance of sturdy links with key individuals, is bound to have a positive influence on their governments and public opinion. Many possibilities and potentials open up if we but take a pragmatic approach. I call this "pragmatic diplomacy," and I believe that as long as this approach is maintained, Taiwan will continue to exist.

It is true that in the past visas could be issued only when diplomatic relations existed between states. But there is nothing wrong with yielding this authority to the Taipei Representative Office or the Taipei Economic and Cultural Office in countries that have no diplomatic ties with us. The important thing is to guarantee the existence of Taiwan and to strengthen that existence.

This existence as the premise of foreign relations is expressed in the accompanying diagram. The vertical axis denotes relations with the mainland, with promotion of cross-strait relations at the top and of independence for Taiwan at the bottom. On the horizontal axis, which represents foreign relations, development of pragmatic foreign policy lies to the right and international isolation to the left. The first (upper right) quadrant represents the vector of balanced, peaceful solutions; the second (upper left) quadrant represents unification, accepting the conditions of the mainland; the third (lower left) quadrant, independence and international isolation; and the fourth (lower right) quadrant, realistic foreign relations giving top priority to Taiwanese independence.

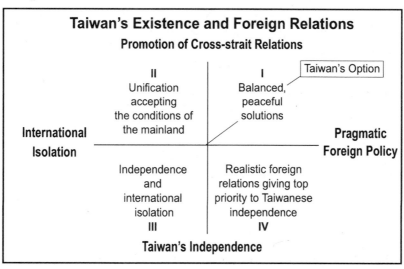

It goes without saying that, given the situation today, we have no other option than that of the most balanced conditions, promoting relations between Taiwan and the continent and pursuing pragmatic diplomacy. This is the only means to avoid forced unification by Communist China or isolation in the international community. The problem is the disparity between quadrant I and quadrant IV. Should independence be stressed? Should relations with the continent be maintained? Certainly this is very tricky terrain in which to maneuver, and plotting a safe course is by no means easy. It is also necessary to alert domestic public opinion to the trade-offs involved in this endeavor.

If, however, we remain cognizant of the basic importance of existence for Taiwan, we need not vacillate. What we need to do is to secure internal stability that is absolutely necessary for social and economic development. In the long term, Taiwan will develop internally, and its relations with other countries will grow still broader and closer. That will allow Taiwan to assert its existence even more positively.

## Challenging the Global Standard

This approach to foreign affairs is something that is needed in the pursuit of global standards in business as well. In Japan, we find both those with a tendency to worship global standards and those who deliberately avoid them as smacking too much of the "American standard."

Global standards, however, really ought to be considered in broader perspective. We need to think of them as criteria that will contribute to a new world order, albeit one that is not yet complete. First of all, there continue to be countries in the world that follow the communist banner, and we must not forget that they have not yet cast aside their allegiance to their own type of order. Second, we must keep in mind that even countries that have adopted liberal democracy have not solved problems stemming from ethnic or religious differences.

We must also keep an observant eye on what is happening in Europe, the birthplace of democracy. Since instituting a common currency among the members of the European Union in 1999,

Europe is on the way to creating yet another order on the threshold of the twenty-first century.

The global standard that the United States calls on the world to adopt consists of a free market economy and democratic government. However, this is simply the scheme the United States envisions in its plan for the formation of a U.S.–centered new world order. Not only other countries but the United States itself should recognize its inherent biases. If the United States purports to be the leader of the new world order, it ought to be more considerate of the sensibilities of the countries that give allegiance to freedom and democracy. If it ignores the voices of other democratic countries, it will not be able to maintain any sort of new order.

In the autumn of 1998, while Japan's Diet was in the process of debating a bill to revive its faltering banks and other financial institutions, Prime Minister Obuchi Keizo paid an official visit to the United States for talks with President Bill Clinton. On that occasion, it is said that Clinton told Obuchi that the Japanese government ought to appropriate public funds in order to rescue the banks that were failing as a result of their so-called bad loans. If the United States is going to make such demands on Japan, it ought to be ready to offer some financial or other incentive. Mr. Obuchi would have been justified, I believe, in asking for funding assistance for that purpose.

Insofar as the global standard represents the formation of a new world order, it behooves the leader of that order to actively participate in and support its formation with pecuniary and other resources. The same is true in the world of business. Toyota

Motors president Okuda Hiroshi has proposed a hybrid car designed to protect the earth's environment as a new, global standard model. This kind of original endeavor aimed at contributing to the formation of the international order is sorely needed.

No doubt the way the United States responds to the attempt to make the hybrid car fit global standards will provide an excellent barometer of what the international order of the future will be like.

### Taiwan in the New World Order

When considering the kinds of problems inherent in global standards in the area of business, let us look first at a very obvious example of something that happened in the European Community.

A certain German company wanted to import a French liqueur called "crème de cassis." However, there is a law in Germany that prohibits the import of liqueurs that contain over a certain percentage of alcohol, so the German order had to be canceled. The French liqueur manufacturer, however, filed a lawsuit against Germany in the European Court of Justice. It felt justified because the European court ruled that the Germans could not block a product that was already sold in France, except for health, fair trade, consumer protection, or fiscal reasons. The court placed the onus for demonstrating evidence of violation of "health, fair trade, consumer protection, or fiscal reasons" on the German side, and from that time on it became the rule between Germany and France: "If there are differences among products that are based on nonessential requirements, there must be 'mutual recognition' of national regulations and industrial standards."

In participating in international organizations or conventions that set global standards, the same kinds of problems are constantly surfacing. No matter what kind of international standards there are, none are adopted without some measure of friction. Those who decide to agree to such standards, moreover, must adopt due measures to deal with the problems that may result. For example, should Taiwan become a member of the World Trade Organization (WTO) as envisioned in the near future, it must accept a number of obligations that accompany that membership, and these could create major problems for Taiwan as it is today.

In Taiwan, for example, alcoholic beverages had always been manufactured and distributed by a government monopoly. Income from the sale of alcohol was considerable, but the industry could not develop further in that sector. Furthermore, monopoly on all sales made it difficult to import alcoholic beverages from Europe and the United States. We therefore ended the government monopoly and handed over production and distribution to private enterprise, imposing a tax in exchange.

We were concerned, at first, that liquor products from overseas would flood into the market, dealing a heavy blow to domestic producers. As it turned out, however, most of the competition from the United States consisted of California wines, from the U.K. Scotch whisky, and from France brandy and wine, and the effect on local producers of traditional liquor products was negligible.

Of course, Taiwan itself produces wine and brandy, and great deal of money and effort was invested in order to put these products on a commercial basis. Our local wines and brandies will continue to be sold as gourmet wines and liquors. It is certain, however, that once the market is liberalized and foreign goods begin to flow into Taiwan, it will no longer be possible to market them as they once were.

### Nothing Ventured, Nothing Gained

Import of agricultural products involved major problems. If we allowed pork and chicken meat to be freely imported, the farms would be hard hit. We have submitted a request to the WTO that exceptions be made for such products as are made for rice in the case of Japan, but at the same time, we have created a relief fund for affected farmers. The fund is roughly NT$21 billion but needs to be increased to at least NT$100 billion.

The real threat posed by liberalization of the meat market revolves around pork and poultry viscera. Internal parts of pork and chicken are especially prized in Taiwanese cuisine. There is high demand for them, and local farmers rely on them as an important source of income.

In the United States, on the other hand, while meat viscera is used to a certain extent in the manufacture of sausage, it is not in high demand, and on the whole pork bellies and poultry offal are discarded. Should the Taiwan meat market be flooded by imported meat products, the blow to local pork and chicken farmers would be obvious. Under such circumstances, local farmers would be quickly reduced to penury without some degree of government compensation. We have to consider carefully how serious the impact of liberalization of farm products will be on local farmers, and estimate what level of subsidy relief will be necessary while looking ahead to gauge the degree of social change that can be expected to occur.

Responses to global standards vary, of course, depending a great deal on conditions in each country, especially their political and economic strengths. I do not think that Japan should feel it necessary to shun global standards; it has ample strength with which to deal with the challenges, and considering its political and military ties with the United States it does not seem a wise juncture to reject the American call.

In fact, it would be to Japan's advantage to champion the idea of global standards and actually take the lead, rather than adopting a passive or negative stance. As we say in Chinese, "If you do not enter the tiger's den, you will not catch the tiger's cub," which is to say, "Nothing ventured, nothing gained." Japan should courageously venture into international society and present its demands in a forthright manner. Japan is sure only to grow stronger for having "entered the tiger's den." In the case of Taiwan, it will not be that difficult to make the necessary adjustments in industry. The challenge will be for agriculture. To deal with such eventualities, we must make careful preparations and do our best to reach international levels in the agricultural sector.

## Education Paves the Way for the Future

The people of Taiwan are traditionally devoted to education. Until very recently the Constitution stipulated that 15 percent of the central government budget should be earmarked for education and culture. When legislators amended this part of the charter to remove the 15 percent stipulation, there was much opposition, with vehement demonstrations protesting what they assumed was a "reduction" of public investment in education.

These protests themselves were an indication of how important people consider education, although the removal of the 15 percent figure was meant not to decrease government spending on education and culture but to build in greater budgetary flexibility. As a matter of fact, because Taiwan's GNP had drastically increased, investment in education and culture had become inflated; even after eliminating the 15 percent target, the budgetary amount in this category may be above the amount that percentage represents. I cannot imagine any other country that spends as much on education as Taiwan does today.

The 15 percent stipulation, moreover, simply covered the proportion of the central government budget being spent on education, and local governments as well set aside ample amounts. The fact that educational expenses through the junior high school level are supported entirely by local governments represents a considerable investment in the future by Taiwan as a whole.

Taiwan also plans to invest a total of NT$175 billion in educational reforms through the revision of textbooks and the expansion of educational resources, teaching staff, and facilities. One aspect of these reforms pertains to foreign-language education. In the case of English-language education, for example, students do not progress satisfactorily when they begin only to study from the seventh grade. The development of the language-acquisition part of the brain is greatest at a very early age, hence bilingual education can benefit by starting early. If such study begins after the brain has developed beyond a certain point, as has been scientifically demonstrated, the links between the parts of the brain coordinating different languages will be much weaker. By learning Taiwanese, Mandarin Chinese, and English from the primary school years, children will enjoy great facility not only in communication but also in creative thinking and imagination.

Taiwan plans to hire a large number of young teachers to carry out this plan. The salaries of veteran teachers on the verge of retirement are high. Since the salaries of younger instructors are relatively lower, it will be possible to give older teachers ample severance allowances for early retirement, thereby opening the way for an infusion of new blood and new teaching methods in the new century.

Also included in the educational reforms is the promotion of education of the "heart" or "spirit." This education of the spirit will be greatly needed in Taiwan from now on. Taiwan is certainly more affluent than it ever was, and progress has been made in democratization, yet deviance of many kinds has erupted throughout our society.

Developments in the industrially advanced nations have shown how the achievement of affluence in society can bring on the contrary phenomena of psychological anxiety and decay of the spirit. In particular, the heightening of self-awareness seems to be accompanied by a diminishing sense of responsibility toward society. Some of the same symptoms are beginning to appear in Taiwan, too.

Advances in the economy, moreover, have allowed profiteering and speculation to run rampant, threatening to overwhelm people's feelings of mutual tolerance and respect for others, sentiments that are indispensable for the nurture of a democratic society. Virtues that have been treasured in our traditional culture — diligence, frugality, integrity, and kindness — are threatened by the allure of fame, power, and wealth.

To combat this trend, which I call the "crisis of the spirit," I advocate what we call "spiritual revitalization." This is aimed, starting with the individual person, at instituting measures of all kinds—in educational reform, administrative reform, social restructuring, and promotion of culture—in the endeavor to restore the health of society, honor social justice, and revive ethical standards. Through these reforms, we seek development that can strike a balance between tradition and modernity and between the spiritual and the material.

### The Need for New Textbooks
The long-established system of entrance examinations to senior high schools has imposed a heavy burden on Taiwan's children. Beginning in 2001, these entrance examinations will be abolished and replaced with a unified junior–senior high school system.

In the new system there will be no examinations for continuing from elementary to junior high school, and for those who do not go on to senior high school, there will be vocational education programs. We will also make it possible for those who have finished vocational school to attend university if they wish.

The new plans for education are premised on the recognition

of individual differences in human development. Some children mature early, others take more time to develop. It will not be possible to educate all children without adjusting our approaches to deal with each and every type of child.

We are also keenly aware of the need to revise our school textbooks.

During my term as vice-president of the Republic of China, I read through all of Taiwan's elementary and junior high school textbooks for Chinese literature, arithmetic/mathematics, history, and other subjects, and have been very concerned about them ever since. I was aghast at what I found.

For example, in the textbooks for instruction in Chinese, there is not one mention of any of the great figures of other countries. The names of people like George Washington, Isaac Newton, or Albert Einstein are nowhere to be seen. This situation is not likely to foster a people with an international outlook.

Arithmetic textbooks as well do not seem to be written with real children in mind. They dwell too much on some subjects and skip to advanced problems too abruptly. I met with the educators involved and expressed my belief that revisions should be made. I told them I thought the arithmetic textbooks were making life miserable for children. Up to fourth grade, they looked all right, but from fifth grade the material suddenly became very difficult. Even if pupils liked arithmetic up until fourth grade, I complained, they would come to loathe the subject in fifth grade using those texts.

At first the teachers seemed to be taken by surprise at the details I cited to illustrate my point. But then they admitted that they, in fact, had long been aware of the problem.

Our history textbooks, too, should no longer revolve around the history of the Nationalist Party but cover the history of Taiwan itself. The story of the native peoples who have lived on the island since antiquity and of the successive waves of immigrants that came from various places, as well as how the Taiwan of today was built, must be fully and accurately told; the process by which the island began to appear in the histories of ancient times and how it became widely known; the influences it felt from the continent during the Ming dynasty starting in the fifteenth century; how the name "Taiwan" came into use in the sixteenth century; how the Portuguese named the island Formosa; and how Cheng Ch'eng-kung attempted to restore the Ming dynasty from his base in Taiwan.

Taiwan came to be inhabited by many peoples arriving on its shores at different periods over the centuries. The story of Taiwan's history from the time of the Ch'ing dynasty through the period of Japanese rule from 1895 to 1945 needs to be told in a well-balanced fashion in our textbooks. Particularly since a generation is becoming active on the political stage that did not experience the complicated events since the end of World War II and do not have firsthand knowledge of the February 28 Incident of 1947, we must provide a fair and accurate account of this phase of history.

## Judicial Reform as Condition for Democratization

I have already mentioned some of the administrative changes undertaken in our pursuit of democratization, but the area of reform that is most crucial to our goal of joining the company of mature democratic states in the world is the judiciary. A democratic state must also be governed by the rule of law. In the absence of a well-established legal system, the discretion of government or persons in power is unchecked, bringing the momentum of democratization to a standstill. Anyone who has studied law in the advanced nations would probably be quite amazed to know what the judicial system of Taiwan has been like up until now. Of the many branches of law, take, for example, the law of civil procedure. In most countries there is a massive body of detailed regulations for the enforcement of the civil code, but for the approximately 640 articles of the Republic of China's Code of Civil Procedure, there are only twelve articles in the Enforcement Law of Civil Procedure.

In contrast, there are as many as eighty "Internal Guidelines on Implementation of Civil Procedure." Although I have called for the revision of this system for a long time, few people have supported me. Leaving things the way they are permits more discretionary freedom, giving judges and prosecutors a freer hand to do what they want.

However, once such discretionary decisions should come to bear in court cases, they impair justice and can no longer be called "law." Discretion is exercised on the basis of the "Internal Guidelines" only and does not represent the voice of the people. Under this system, too, the interests of the people are not duly heeded.

For the advancement of democracy in Taiwan and for our creation of the next stage of the "Taiwan experience," legal reform is sorely needed. If reform of education represents the re-birth of individuals, reform of the legal system is equivalent to the rebirth of society. Without reform of both, Taiwan's demo-cratization will not advance and the future will not be ours.

Nevertheless, as is the case with any country, change is some-thing extremely difficult to engineer in the realm of law. No matter how vehemently I argue, those who preside over the law in Taiwan are reluctant to take action. Over and over I was told that "there is much opposition, and nothing can be done."

I reassure them that it does not matter if there is some oppo-sition. We must listen to all opposing views and list them up. A consensus might still be achieved regarding some of them.

There were, in fact, many voices opposing the revision of the Constitution in 1997. After I was reelected president in 1996, I had meetings of the National Development Council held at the district level and asked members to vote on the revision of the Constitution. Those opinions were brought to the central Coun-cil and deliberated in a preliminary session to achieve some con-sensus before being presented to the plenary session. Opinions that did not obtain a consensus were recorded as individual opin-ions. Proceeding in this fashion, we were able to encourage op-ponents to come forward and express their views. As a result, we implemented only the proposals that gained consensus and moved on smoothly.

No progress will be made in legal reform by emphasizing the opposition alone. It is already perfectly clear that the present legal system can no longer keep pace with Taiwan as it is today.

## Stronger Infrastructure and Further Reform

Something we cannot forget as we endeavor to sustain Taiwan's economic development is the importance of improving social overhead capital. When we were inspecting our electric power industry we discovered a very large facility that had been left idle. Investigation revealed that it had not been in use for more than ten years. It had been deemed no longer essential.

From my point of view, however, even though the facility might not be needed for the electric power industry, it could certainly be used for other related projects. As a matter of fact, given the location of the facility, it could be put to very beneficial use. I immediately took steps to encourage the persons responsible to put the equipment and the site to good use.

Today one of Taiwanese enterprises' greatest woes is the difficulty of finding suitable locations for their facilities. In the wake of rapid development, good sites have become extremely hard to find. Sometimes, as in the case above, the land is actually there. It may simply be taken up by a now-outdated facility whose role has come to an end and which has become a kind of blind spot because it is such an established part of the scenery. One enterprise that has taken the initiative in this regard is the Taiwan Sugar Corporation. A state enterprise, Taiwan Sugar no longer engages in the cultivation of sugar cane except on a small scale. Since it owns some 50,000 hectares of land, however, it has freed 18,000 hectares for other uses.

I had proposed a plan for government-subsidized worker housing and announced that I wanted to sell the housing at NT$60,000 per *ping* (36 square feet). Taiwan Sugar came forward and the joint venture turned out to be extremely timely.

The problem, however, came from people in the construction industry who complained that it was not fair to build cheap government subsidized housing while they were unable to sell the houses they had already built. Looked at only from one perspective, one can see how construction companies might feel betrayed. However, since success in projects like this can lend momentum to the construction business as a whole, recently the opposition has grown quiet.

As these examples illustrate, what is needed in terms of social overhead capital changes from one phase to the next. In formulating policy, therefore, the government must be certain to look well into the future and gauge the way things are going to be. Taiwan has not reached the point where we can simply leave development up to the private sector.

# CHAPTER **4**

# Washington, Peking, and Taipei

D RAMATIC CHANGES have been taking place in mainland China. During the past two decades, with steady economic growth and the partial open-door policy, the appalling disaster of the Cultural Revolution is finally fading from people's memories. I am happy that their material lives have improved considerably and that some leeway is beginning to emerge in their thinking and attitudes as well. I do not stint in praise for the mainland today in these respects.

In observing the rapidly changing international situation, however, I believe we must obtain a more comprehensive grasp of conditions in mainland China apart from reports of isolated incidents, figures found in official statistics, and impressions of travelers and tourists. While it is encouraging to hear that people in the mainland now enjoy better and more peaceful lives, we should be careful not to become too optimistic about conditions there. Neither should we give up all hope out of excessive pessimism and misinformation. Rather, we need to be able to assess the actual situation in mainland China and in Taiwan and objectively compare the two.

The reforms we are seeing on the Chinese mainland have been mainly structural, but recently the Communist regime's effort to engineer controlled change has reached a dead-end. Although the changes being made seem dramatic, they do not necessarily alter the basic structures. The mainland has increased industrial production, but politically it remains under the autocratic single-party rule of the Chinese Communist Party (CCP). There is no change in the situation of a dictatorship by a few. The CCP itself has not changed its essential character or political stance except in the surrender of complete state authority over the economy.

Grave contradictions pervade a system that is leftist politically and rightist economically, a system that is communist politically but follows the principles of the market economy. A better livelihood makes people feel more or less satisfied for the time being, but if the basic contradictions remain unresolved, confusion will inevitably ensue and become uncontrollable.

After two decades of change in the quantitative dimension, the mainland has now reached a crucial point from which to proceed to qualitative change. According to forecasts made by U.S. and other analysts, the mainland will probably need another twenty years to deal with the contradictions and map a pathway to genuine change. But is that really possible? If it is, what are the conditions that will make it so?

## Change on an Unprecedented Scale

Seen from the other side of the Taiwan Strait, structural change would seem very difficult to achieve in mainland China. The United States estimates it will take twenty years, but I suspect much more time will be needed as the situation now stands. Even if a certain degree of change is attained, it will not go smoothly, as suggested by events in Russia over the last ten years.

Let us look briefly at the problems the mainland has to overcome in order to institute basic structural change. First of all, the mainland is full of uncertainty. Without eliminating at least some of the unknowns, radical change cannot be achieved. The sources of uncertainty include institutional contradictions, the slow pace of democratization, and the absence of a government based on the rule of law. These uncertainties not only affect the policy making of the CCP but heightens the risk of developments that may be beyond the power of the authorities to resolve. In order to prevent turmoil that the Peking authorities themselves might not be able to control, the United States has been trying to enhance stability in and around mainland China through diplomatic negotiations and economic assistance. These efforts may be of some use, but they cannot make a decisive difference.

Second, the structural changes the Chinese mainland has to undertake will be unprecedented in scale. The territory involved is vast and its population is huge. The problems are further compounded by the extraordinary, as well as deep-rooted, cultural and social diversity of mainland China. It seems overoptimistic to think that reform on this vast a scale can be completed within a couple of decades. Long-term reforms will be needed, and there is no time to waste in carrying them out, given the rapid changes occurring in the region as a whole.

Third, mainland China's relations with neighboring countries are extremely unstable. For the sake of the welfare of people on the mainland, international friction needs to be avoided wherever possible. Strained relations with Taiwan could pose a threat to the hard-won economic prosperity that has finally emerged on the mainland. Peking, therefore, should exercise prudence in its relations across the Strait.

## Patient, Steady Improvement of Relations
If these problems are weighed, it is not difficult for Taiwan to determine what course it should take. Comparing the mainland

and Taiwan helps us to know what to do. The mainland, huge though it is, remains more or less closed and autocratic, and although the people are economically better off, the territory and population are too large for everyone to enjoy prosperity. The government, furthermore, is belligerent and hegemonic, relentless in its threatening attitude toward Taiwan. By contrast, Taiwan is not large in area, but it enjoys widespread economic prosperity. It is steadily building an increasingly open and democratic system. It has formed solid ties with many countries and has established a firm place for itself in the international community through peaceful means. It will continue to be active in this endeavor.

Taiwan's policy toward Peking could change tremendously if the mainland ceased to be antagonistic toward Taipei and took steps to eliminate some of its own uncertainties. As things stand now, the most desirable posture is one of patient, unhurried effort. I believe other countries would agree. The greatest concern, I repeat, are the many uncertainties in developments on the mainland.

From long ago there was an oft-repeated slogan that "The Han and the rebels cannot stand together." In other words, the Han people (i.e., the Nationalist Party) and the rebels (the Communists) cannot compromise. But Taiwan discarded this idea long ago in favor of the quest for a "win-win" situation for China as a whole. It no longer seeks the demise of the mainland Chinese regime. Taiwan has shown its readiness to cooperate with the mainland if there are things that can be improved in dealings across the Strait. It has advanced many specific proposals, such as summit meetings, joint international projects, the building of an offshore transportation center, cultural exchange, agricultural cooperation, and reform of state-run enterprises.

Unfortunately, almost none of these well-intentioned proposals have been carried out. The leaders of the mainland remain belligerent. Clinging rigidly to their idea of "one China," they seek to incorporate Taiwan into that "one-China" framework, conducting propaganda campaigns based on the information—which is groundless—that Taiwan will take forcible measures to gain independence. Because of that, our win-win idea cannot be put into action, which has forced us to maintain the "patience over haste, steady progress for the long term" policy.

When I meet China experts from the United States, I say to them, "I hope Washington understands and supports our 'one-China' policy." What is important is that it is *our* one-China policy, not the mainland's. It is our hope that Washington understands and agrees to *our* one-China policy. The United States should not easily agree to the mainland's one-China policy, however. The United States would also be mistaken if it promotes its Taiwan policy on the basis of the false information that Taiwan is pursuing a policy aimed at independence.

Taiwan's policy has been and continues to be the promotion of cross-strait dialogue and the improvement of relations with the mainland. Rather than responding to our goodwill with reciprocity, Communist China has continually isolated Taiwan in the international arena by quashing our space for international activities. Peking has used its "one-China" policy to claim that it is a central government while we are a local government, thereby undermining and obscuring the Republic of China's status as an independent and sovereign state. Nothing could be further from the truth. The Republic of China was established as an independent sovereign state in 1912, long before the People's Republic of China was founded in 1949. Throughout its history, the PRC has never had jurisdiction over the Taiwan area, even for a day; the ROC is not its local government. To let such a gross fallacy continue would further create misconceptions in the international community and difficulties for Taiwan in its economic development, international relations, and even cross-strait dialogue. It is therefore important for the world to recognize the existence of the Republic of China on Taiwan, an independent and sovereign state since its founding in 1912. Peking should also face the reality that there are two equals on either side of the Taiwan Strait.

## "One Country, Two Systems" Rejected

I expressed these ideas straightforwardly at the closing of the National Unification Council meeting on July 22, 1998. Although a bit long, let me cite part of that speech because it has historical significance. What follows is a summary of my remarks:

> We must take this opportunity to once again state clearly and solemnly: China must be reunified. However, this reunification must be under a system of democracy, freedom, and equitable prosperity that will safeguard the rights and interests of all Chinese, and is in keeping with the global trend. The nation should, by no means, be reunified under the proven failure of communism or the so-called "one country, two systems" formula.
>
> Our position on this issue is firmly grounded in our beliefs

that: First, reunification under communism or the "one country, two systems" formula will not help bring democracy to the whole of China. Instead, it will drive the people of the mainland farther away from their aspirations to enjoy a democratic way of life. Second, only if China is reunified under a democratic system can the strengths of Taiwan, Hong Kong, and the Chinese mainland be forged together as a force for regional stability. A reunified China that is closed and autocratic would necessarily provoke anxiety in neighboring countries, upset the power balance in Asia, and threaten the peace and stability of the Asia–Pacific region. Third, only the implementation of a comprehensive democratic system, through the rule of law and transparent political processes will mutual trust be enhanced between the two sides. And only democracy will ensure that both sides in fact honor their agreements and guarantee a new win-win situation.

Once again, we resolutely reject the so-called one-country, two-systems scheme. It has a number of fundamental flaws, the first of which is ambiguity. While the formula seems to offer two equal systems, it in fact makes a very unequal distinction between central and local. The formula is also contradictory, for it seeks to wed communism with capitalism. Finally, the "one country, two systems" model is undemocratic; power is exercised from the top down, not from the bottom up. This runs completely counter to the democratic reunification that we seek.

In this speech I rejected the "one country, two systems" idea that holds that communism and capitalism can coexist in continental China. This notion is confounded by its own inherent contradictions, and it is very far from the objectives to which we aspire.

## Six Points

In that same speech, I also listed six matters that we wish the PRC to appreciate in its dealings with Taiwan.

First, although there will be only one China in the future, at present there is one divided China. The Republic of China was established in 1912, and although the government moved to Taiwan in 1949, the Peking authorities have never exercised jurisdiction over Taiwan. That the two sides of the Taiwan Strait are ruled by two separate political entities is an objective fact that cannot be denied.

Second, the reunification of China should proceed in a gradual and orderly fashion. When the conditions are ripe, success will come naturally. No timetable need be set. The pace of democratization on the Chinese mainland and the improvement of cross-strait relations will decide the progress toward peaceful reunification.

Third, prior to reunification, the people of the Republic of China on Taiwan should possess the right to full self-defense. This is the inherent right of the 21.8 million people in Taiwan. It is also necessary to preserve the achievements of democratic reform in the Taiwan area and encourage democratic change on the Chinese mainland.

Fourth, in light of the needs for survival and development, the people of the Republic of China on Taiwan should enjoy the right to participate in international activities as they did in the 1950s and 1960s. This way, the people on both sides will have equal opportunity to contribute to the international community.

Fifth, Taiwan and the mainland should expand exchanges and enhance the prosperity of both. Cooperation should replace antagonism, and reciprocity should dissolve animosity. In this fashion, a propitious foundation can be laid for the future peaceful reunification of China.

Finally, the two sides should pursue full communication on the principles of equality and mutual respect in order to resolve differences and seek common ground. They should hold consultations based on the reality of a divided China and sign a cross-strait peace agreement, thereby ending the state of hostility, promoting harmony in cross-strait relations, and preserving the stability of the Asia–Pacific region.

As clearly stated in this speech, our policy toward mainland China is to engage in dialogue on the basis of parity and equality. We seek to resume negotiations to resolve the host of issues that arise from economic, cultural, and educational interaction as well as tourism and other people-to-people exchanges. Our long-term goal is peaceful unification of China under the principles of democracy, freedom, and equitable prosperity for all.

## True Meaning of the "Taiwan Experience"
I have emphasized Taiwan's achievements in this volume, but not because they represent the consequence of a long history of liberal democracy. Indeed, it is only over the last half century since the end of World War II that Taiwan has built the political, economic, and social systems we see today. What I want to do is to share our experience with my fellow Chinese on the mainland and with the world.

When the Republic of China moved to Taiwan, neither prosperity nor peace and order prevailed on the island. The initial rule of the Kuomintang (KMT) was authoritarian, even dictatorial, it is true. Violence was committed by some in power, and there was suppression of the indigenous people of Taiwan and the descendants of early settlers by those who crossed the Strait with the KMT. Later, Taiwan developed economically, its social conditions stabilized, and political democratization progressed, as symbolized by the adoption of direct presidential elections.

It should be obvious to everyone that the Republic of China has brought economic, social, and political development to Taiwan, and that the achievements of successive political leaders have accumulated over the years. This experience of people of the same ethnic and cultural backgrounds should provide a more suitable model for people on the mainland attempting to achieve democratization than the experience of people anywhere else in the world.

Chinese culture and social institutions have done much to impede the progress of Chinese society, as mentioned in Chapter one, but that is not the whole story. On the contrary, the Chinese can achieve economic prosperity while stepping firmly along the path of democracy. Taiwan's experience testifies to that.

Much of our experience in Taiwan should be readily understood by people on the mainland. Taking a close look at Taiwan, they ought to realize the fundamental and serious contradictions inherent in the course their government is pursuing. The "Taiwan experience," or the "Taiwan model," is not for the people in Taiwan alone but for all Chinese. It will be an essential model for the reunified China. Only then, and I say this with special emphasis, will the Taiwan experience assume its true significance.

We therefore cannot assent to the one-China formula that is so high-handedly upheld by the PRC authorities, although we do earnestly hope that the partial attempts at democratization they are currently engaging in at the village level will succeed. We also want to see the mainland introduce political reforms and expand the breadth and depth of democratization so that our fellow Chinese on the continent will be able to fully apply their ingenuity and abilities in building a multifaceted and open modern society.

**The Essence of the "Quiet Revolution"**
The problems that mainland China must overcome are, needless to say, far greater in scale and more serious than those for Taiwan. I recognize that the difficulties Taiwan had prior to the reforms are not comparable to the problems now confronting the mainland in diversity, complexity, and gravity. The bigger and more serious the problems, however, the greater will be the miseries perpetrated by misguided policies. When a policy line is flawed, it could result in a disaster that involves all of the PRC's Asian neighbors as well.

If we recall the process of Taiwan's reforms, we will note that farsightedness and able planning of political leaders over the decades are responsible for the splendid results of current government policy. Had the leaders charted a fundamentally wrong course and failed to deal squarely with the problems they faced, the government would not be able to pursue the policies it does today. Had the people of Taiwan not responded willingly to the measures adopted by their political leaders, they would not have matured as the democratic citizens who form the support base of government today.

It may be said that the people of Taiwan were "reborn" as a new breed of citizen. A lethargic populace under an authoritarian regime was transformed into an energetic citizenry under democratic government. One should not forget, however, that this change was accomplished gradually over half a century. A democratic citizenry is not something suddenly conceived of one day and achieved the next. Neither is it a process that can be brought about through violent revolution.

In retrospect, the process Taiwan underwent could be called "revolutionary," but it took half a century. It occurred under sustained economic growth and social stability. The rapid structural change that has taken place over the last ten years or so—the change in which I myself was deeply involved—was also a "quiet revolution." This revolution was in essence an inconspicuous, ceaseless endeavor pursued in four areas: political democratization, pragmatic foreign policy, closer relations across the Strait, and the upgrading of the economy. The first three were new developments born through the quiet revolution. Until then, economic development had been Taiwan's foremost priority. It had been believed that as long as the economy improved, other problems could be handled. This belief proved correct to some extent. However, with tremendous changes occurring in the international environment and with new developments in the mainland, political reforms have become all the more important for Taiwan.

The greatest challenge for people of Taiwan's next generation is how to further progress in the three noneconomic areas, that is, democratization, pragmatic foreign policy, and closer relations with the mainland. It is for this reason that I have tried to write in as much detail as possible about how my generation understood the issues in these three areas and coped with them. Success or failure in these challenges will determine the future not just of Taiwan but of all the Chinese people.

## Substantive Ties of International Relations

Taiwan's existence and development is a unique case in the history of international relations; therefore, its status must be viewed from its realistic contributions to the world rather than from the traditional perspectives of international law. A statistic that is immediately indicative of the position of Taiwan today is the dramatic increase in the number of foreign workers over the past decade. Most of the estimated more than 200,000 workers are from Thailand, Malaysia, Indonesia, and the Philippines. Smaller numbers also come from Myanmar and Bangladesh. If each worker supports a family of five (either in Taiwan or in the home country), we may surmise that Taiwan thus supports the livelihood of about one million people from other parts of Asia. I have heard that there are some 8,000 workers from Nicaragua, and others from Paraguay. No doubt Taiwan's relations with Latin America can be expected to grow closer.

Taiwan today is well equipped to actively accept workers from overseas. Improvements are being instituted to streamline acquisition of entry visas, lengthen the duration of stay, assure health checkups, and provide for national health insurance coverage. Until recently the duration of stay for foreign persons on a working visa was two years, but the maximum time limit has been extended to three years.

Most people entering Taiwan to work from Asia and Latin America are blue-collar laborers. Professionals—lawyers, accountants, and English teachers—are increasing in number, especially from the United States. At the request of the U.S. Department of Commerce, restrictions on the entry of professionals have been eased. It is said that some people apply to come to study the Chinese language while their real purpose is to work in Taiwan as English instructors. It is not as easy as it once was to keep track of the exact purposes of entry.

In addition, Taiwan cooperates with former socialist countries of Eastern Europe in their endeavors to introduce the market economy through private-level human-resource training. We also welcome people who seek to do research on Taiwan's economic development. Since it is very difficult to train financial personnel in countries with little experience in finance, more and more people are coming to Taiwan to receive on-the-job training in banking and securities transactions.

These new circumstances, transcending the question of whether or not Taiwan is a member of the United Nations or has sovereign power, are helping to further validate Taiwan's existence. International relations can be strengthened by forging substantive ties such as described above.

Taiwan also acts as an intermediary in various ways between industrially advanced nations, on the one hand, and countries that have just begun to pursue economic development, on the other. It serves as a crossroad in the Asian region, and a bridge connecting various parts of the world.

## Undercurrent of U.S. Policy toward Taiwan

The heightened presence of Taiwan resulting from its role in the region has not only encouraged the mainland to reconsider its Taiwan policy but also served to stimulate the development effort of many other countries. Supporters of Taiwan around the world have found the recent ambiguity toward Taiwan by the United States the source of unsettling concern.

Ito Kiyoshi, professor of East Asian studies at Kyorin University in Tokyo, in a discussion with me published in the October 1998 issue of the Japanese opinion journal, *Bungei Shunju*, mentioned his concern about U.S. President Bill Clinton's three-noes policy toward Taiwan. During his trip to mainland China, Clinton said no to "two Chinas (the mainland and Taiwan)," the "independence of Taiwan," and "Taiwan's joining U.N. organizations." Ito argued that this three-noes policy could threaten the existence of Taiwan.

Basically, I have confidence in the United States. Washington has openly supported the leaders of the Nationalist Party over the decades and has made the survival of Taiwan an important political priority. In 1979, the United States recognized the People's Republic of China, and ended its diplomatic relations with the Republic of China, but at the same time, it adopted a domestic law, "Taiwan Relations Act," to help secure the security or the economic or social system of the people of Taiwan. This act gives the U.S. president and Congress the right to take appropriate action in response to threats to these interests, such as a military incident on the Taiwan Strait. That is why, in a case such as occurred in 1996, when the mainland conducted missile tests in the Strait, the United States did not sit by silently, but took action to stand by this law.

As mentioned earlier, it is not unusual for U.S. policy toward mainland China to swing delicately back and forth depending on the relations between Congress and the administration. This is a familiar pattern in Washington itself, and so, even when Washington indicates no support for Taiwan, it does not mean that it opposes the policies held by Taipei. During his 1998 visit to the Chinese mainland, Clinton did make remarks that included the three-noes policy, but he did not commit it to a written statement.

Before Clinton's mainland China tour, Susan L. Shirk, deputy assistant secretary of state, met with Taiwan's representative in the United States to explain the situation. Even after Clinton's remarks, the United States dispatched American Institute in Taiwan chairman Richard Bush to Taiwan to explain the "three-noes policy." President Clinton's remark did not represent a change in U.S. policy. After his return home, Clinton was criticized by Congress, which demanded an explanation, and a China debate ensued. These procedures of U.S. foreign policy were exactly what I had expected, and to me they demonstrated the candor and soundness of American diplomacy.

Prior to Clinton's visit, moreover, a resolution demanding that the mainland abandon the use of force against Taiwan was adopted in the U.S. House of Representatives by a vote of 410 to

0. After the visit as well, the Senate and the House of Representatives reemphasized U.S. support of Taiwan by a vote of 92 to 0 and 390 to 1, respectively.

James Lilley, U.S. ambassador in the PRC during the Bush administration, once compared Clinton's ambiguous attitude to a "juvenile diplomacy." In the aforementioned interview for the *Bungei Shunju*, I told Professor Ito that there was no need to criticize Clinton, for Washington did not change anything of vital importance. In diplomacy, there may be various shifts back and forth on peripheral issues, but what really matters is commitment on crucial matters.

**Multilayered Relations with U.S.**

The United States, I believe, ultimately wants to see the mainland become a stable power liberalized and democratized as is Taiwan. It may be a long time before that aspiration is realized, but in the meantime, it is important to engage the mainland and have it observe international order somehow. Apart from the question of whether things will unfold as Washington wishes, international stability is what the United States needs now. The worst scenario is that the mainland recklessly moves in a wrong direction and threatens the international order, thereby causing severe damage to the interests of the United States. That is why the United States cannot but adopt a seemingly conflicting policy toward Peking.

A look at U.S. policy toward the mainland and Taiwan shows differences in thinking between the administration and Congress as well as among the various departments. This is only natural.

The U.S. Congress has traditionally been sympathetic to Taiwan. The American people in general are aware that the Chinese regime that advocates freedom and democracy is the Nationalist Party, and that it is Taiwan that has achieved freedom and democracy and shows greater respect for human rights. Within the U.S. administration itself, there are some differences in approach, with one department distancing itself from Taiwan while another stresses Taiwan's vital strategic position, and is not as keen to cooperate or sympathize with the mainland.

These differences are a matter of course. We are fully aware of the multilayered character of U.S. relations vis-à-vis Taiwan, and we must therefore keep up with what is happening.

**Close Private-level Ties**
In addition to relations with the U.S. government, connections that influential American individuals have maintained with Taiwan since the time of President Chiang Kai-shek are also important. When Chiang Kai-shek's son, Chiang Ching-kuo, passed away in 1988, John D. Rockefeller III flew to Taiwan two days later to express his condolences. He and I have been friends since then. He once studied in Japan and can also speak Japanese, so English and Japanese are mingled in our conversation.

Partly because Rockefeller is based in West Virginia, Taiwan chose that state for a joint venture with a U.S. corporation to build an airplane factory. Employing some 900 local workers helped the factory make a significant contribution to the prosperity of the state of West Virginia. In other areas of the United States as well, we have established joint ventures for the manufacture of plastic, microelectronic, and other products. Because of these projects, I have had the opportunity to meet and exchange opinions with many U.S. congressmen and congresswomen. Such acquaintances, formed through working on endeavors of common interest, can prove a valuable source of support.

Taiwan has also sought to build close cultural ties with the United States. Many sister-state and sister-city relations have been set up. When I was mayor of Taipei, I was invited to a mayors' conference in the United States. It was the first time a mayor had been invited from overseas. Ever since then I have cultivated and expanded relations with mayors of various cities in the United States.

We now have a project to invite young Americans to study about Taiwan. To promote this project, we have a guide to Taiwan on the Internet and provide information to American high-school radio broadcasting stations. This effort has yet to come to full fruition. We intend to persevere, however, in the conviction that Taiwan's future depends on whether it is truly understood by young people in the United States.

We also use the Internet for a project to link Taiwanese organizations around the world. There are already Taiwan Chambers of Commerce throughout the world that organize Taiwanese merchants/businesspeople overseas. We are trying to link these organizations, now situated in Japan, Southeast Asia, Central and South America, and Europe, via the Internet. Such Internet connections may change the pattern of their business activities and reveal business opportunities. The joining of this network with Taiwanese banks in New York and elsewhere will create a huge financial network.

### Further Expectations of the United States

Our relations with the United States have grown closer on both the government and private levels, but if asked whether we are satisfied with every U.S. response to Taiwan, we would have to say no.

For example, although the Taiwan Relations Act spells out today's U.S. Taiwan policy, it is obvious that Taiwan must improve its military capabilities in order to enhance the security and stability of the Taiwan Strait region. However, it was not until negotiations for the purchase of Mirage fighter aircraft from France made progress that the United States ceased its reluctance to discuss exporting F-16s to Taiwan. In world military affairs today, Taiwan's strategic position should not be ignored. The currently much-talked-about defense system, Theater Missile Defense (TMD), will be effective in East Asia only if the United States, Japan, and Taiwan participate, at some future time to be joined by the Republic of Korea.

We also want the United States to give more support to Taiwan's efforts to join international organizations, and I believe Taiwan's participation would be to American advantage. For the sake of its reputation, the PRC is determined to take its place in various international organizations before Taiwan does. We hope the United States will help make it possible for Taiwan to join the World Trade Organization, the International Monetary Fund, the World Bank, and other international organizations that do not require United Nations membership as a prerequisite for entry. Obtaining a seat in the United Nations can wait, although it is our final goal. Considering Taiwan's current status in international society, its participation in international organizations is obviously vital in any scheme for a new international order the United States might envision.

I trust the United States in these matters as well. If it does not become confused and adopt unrealistic policies and if Taiwan's international presence does not diminish, I believe the United States will continue to support Taiwan and that Washington's judgment will not err. What I fear, rather, is that Japanese public opinion might misinterpret superficial moves by the United States and the PRC and jump to the conclusion that a major change is occurring. This would be very unfortunate for the United States, Japan, and Taiwan. The possibility of such an over-reaction concerns me. During Clinton's visit to the Chinese mainland, the Japanese media overreacted, and the same sort of thing happened when Jiang Zemin visited Japan. I would like Japanese journalists to be better aware that foreign relations involve both surface currents and deep, strong undercurrents.

# CHAPTER **5**

# Japan's Role
# and
# Responsibilities

As I have stated elsewhere in this book, Japan has been a big influence in my life, and Taiwan as a whole has benefited from Japan in the course of its development. These are realities that warrant recognition.

Many Japanese seem to be very sensitive about the fact that their country once colonized Taiwan. It is clear that making another country a colony and exploiting its land and people are no longer considered good national policies and are not condoned by the ethics of international society today. To dwell on this theme indefinitely, however, is not to the advantage of Japan's future nor is it in the interest of Taiwan.

### Deference to a Fault

Mainland China is bound to make an issue of Japan's actions in China during the war from now on as before. This is part of a deliberate strategy by which it expects to elicit greater amounts of economic assistance, including direct investment from Tokyo. Japan is now well trained: whenever it encounters a problem that involves perceptions of "history," it is quick to consult with the authorities in Peking. Almost without fail some sort of concession will be demanded.

This kind of response has a long tradition in mainland China; the matter of "history" is brought up every time Japan consults it. For every overture Japan makes, Peking can be depended on to make a point of its displeasure.

Prewar Japan had many flaws and made many mistakes, but it did manage to assert itself in the international community. It had pride as the first Asian country to stand up to the Western powers. In the wake of the miscalculations and errors made in the prewar and World War II periods, however, Japan has been plagued throughout the postwar decades by the self-imposed pressure to adopt a low-profile stance toward other countries.

Particularly with regard to mainland China, Japan has been deferential to a fault. It will say yes to virtually anything Peking demands. The bureau staff of Japanese newspapers posted to the mainland cannot write freely about the country for fear that any reports unfavorable to the authorities could result in their being asked to leave or, worse, having the bureau closed. To avoid such a disaster, they check just about everything with the authorities ahead of time. So, of course, they end up reporting only the kind of news that will please the PRC government.

As the story goes, when a television station wants to report news about myself, they make a point of asking mainland China if that will be all right. Even if Peking is to condone such reporting, they will warn that any positive appraisal of Lee Teng-hui will be "problematic."

This weak-kneed position vis-à-vis Peking also posed problems in 1995, when Japan hosted the general meeting of the Asia–Pacific Economic Cooperation group (APEC) in Osaka that year. Before sending out an invitation to me, the Japanese government dispatched a representative to Taiwan to request that "President Lee decline the invitation."

If I am invited to an APEC summit and if I decide that I should go, I will go. Taiwan, after all, is a member of APEC. It is up to me, not Japan or Peking, to determine whether I will attend or not. Japanese today seem unable to see this elementary point. I told the messenger that after I received the invitation I would think of a way that would not put Japan in a difficult position. It was obvious that if I said I would attend, Peking would threaten to boycott the meeting, causing great distress and inconvenience to other APEC members and Japan, the host.

As promised, after I received the invitation, I decided that I would not go after all and appointed an envoy to participate in my stead. Had I accepted the invitation, the host was certain to ask Peking for approval. The PRC's reaction would have presented the Japanese government with an awkward dilemma.

Neither the government nor the media of Japan seem to realize how irregular it is to come and ask me not to attend, or to consult Peking for its opinion. They seem to have forgotten who has the right to make certain decisions. Some say that Japanese behavior reflects the importance of consensus in their society, but even if its intent was to assure a consensus, it seems odd to consult Peking, which had nothing to do with hosting the APEC meeting. The pro-Moscow camp once prevailed in the Japanese media, but later the pro-Peking camp gained a dominance that continues to date. Perhaps it is the latter's influence that is responsible for the strange notion that achieving consensus means getting permission from Peking. Consensus is necessary in international politics, but the "consensus" in the case of the APEC invitation is meaningless and only impedes foreign relations. It should be abandoned. What Japan should do is accurately grasp information on mainland China and behave with greater self-confidence.

## The Yen Should Be Strong

Equally perplexing is Japan's behavior in the realm of international economic policy. Admittedly, economic issues are actually quite complex, but Japan, the world's largest creditor nation, seems too timid in its economic dealings with the world's largest debtor nation, the United States.

The American economy is grounded on the U.S. dollar being the key currency of the world. When necessary, the United States only has to print more greenbacks, but naturally there are limits. If world confidence in the dollar wavered, the American economy might collapse. One recalls the time when Japanese prime minister Hashimoto Ryutaro's remark that he sometimes wished he had had more freedom to sell Japan's holdings of U.S. Treasury notes (federal bonds) sent shock waves through the American business world.

There should be no taboo on selling or not selling U.S. bonds. To be sure, a sudden and massive sale of U.S. bonds could produce the greatest jolt since the Pearl Harbor attack, but it would not pose a problem if Japan only sold some of the U.S. bonds it holds. With this in mind, Japan may call on the United States for financial assistance for Japanese banks struggling to get rid of bad loans. It is understandable that Japanese banks are anxiously working to resolve their bad loans. But, if they try to do this by simply selling their assets, the country's weakened financial market will never recover.

The possibility that Japan's options include a trade-off between borrowing money from the United States and selling U.S. Treasury notes should not be controversial. Washington might not be very happy at first, but Japan should explain its adoption of this option will be to the advantage of the United States and the world economy.

It is often assumed that financiers have excess money to lend to others; therefore, they suffer no financial pressures. Since they make loans to others or invest their money in the endeavors of others, they have every right to use these assets as security to borrow funds necessary to get over their own financial crisis. Politicians in other countries naturally follow this reasoning, but strangely enough, it does not seem to occur to Japanese politicians today.

Of course, not only in the matter of dealing with bad loans but in other issues, the unexpected may happen and plans may go awry. It is the job of politicians to pursue whatever possibilities for solution there may be. Since the bubble of the overheated economy burst, however, Japanese seem to have lost their imagination and flexibility in policy planning.

## Living with a Fiscal Deficit
One is inclined to wonder, too, about some of the arguments advanced in the debate on economic policy in Japan. With regard to domestic demand, a certain Japanese economist argues that, since housing and public facilities have been constructed in ample supply, Japan's economy is in gridlock. Apparently this sort of reasoning makes sense to Japanese.

However, the dwellings standing today need to be replaced sooner or later. It seems to me there are any number of houses that could be rebuilt anew. The argument that the cities are already fully built up sounds plausible enough, but housing and other facilities are actually far from adequate. Modern sewer systems, for example, are not as widely installed in Japan as in the United States and Britain. The furniture and personal effects possessed by Japanese are quite sparse and modest. Few households have the type of furniture and personal possessions that can be considered assets of enduring value. As things stand now, it is hasty to speak of any kind of "saturation." Domestic demand is not necessarily difficult to expand.

In this connection, the fuss over Japan's fiscal deficit a few years ago was quite extraordinary. Data compiled by the Japanese government did indicate a huge deficit in Japan's public coffers, but the situation then was not very serious if compared with that in other major industrial nations, calculated according to the OECD formula. Japanese have obviously grown somewhat oversensitive about the fiscal deficit over the last few years.

In the past Japan skillfully managed to ensure the continued growth of its economy by issuing deficit-bearing national bonds. Today the economy cannot be expected to grow at the same pace, but this does not mean that Japan should sacrifice everything to reduce the deficit. When the economy is in a slump, the deficit will increase somewhat, but this can be made up for in the near future when the economy recovers.

While it discontinued special tax cuts, raised the consumption tax, and curtailed investments in public works projects, the Japanese government tried to boost the economy. Such contradictory policies fail to utilize Japan's great potential.

## Overcoming Gridlock in Japan

When you are attempting to accomplish something, you have to set priorities. Even if the problems at hand are all related, you should not try to solve all of them at once. You should consider what problem to tackle first, what second, and so on in order that their solutions will proceed as smoothly as possible.

It was Japan, after all, that once showed the world how good it was at taking problem solving one step at a time. Today's Japan seems to have forgotten the basic rules of thumb it knew quite well. What caused Japan to end up in this predicament? A major factor is the prevailing hereditary system in Japanese politics. I have high regard for the Japanese people, and often I meet young Japanese who I think would be good leaders if they entered politics. If you know a little about how politicians succeed in Japan, however, you hesitate to encourage promising young people to choose such a career.

Those who want to enter politics in Japan soon find that the fastest way is to be the child of a politician, marry the daughter of a politician, or work as a secretary for a member of the Diet and win his or her favor. It has been more or less demonstrated, however, that this system does not produce really outstanding political leaders. Most of Japan's lawmakers have gained their position in politics in one of these three ways, and this, I would say, is responsible for the lack of vitality in its political world.

Another major factor behind Japan's gridlock is the preeminence of the bureaucracy, which slows the country's response to change. Bureaucrats have grown so powerful that Diet members have ceased to play a meaningful role in formulating policy and drafting legislation, leaving these duties in the hands of ministry officials. As a result, most lawmakers do not even have a clear political philosophy. To make matters worse, bureaucrats have a strong tendency to be preoccupied with narrow jurisdictional concerns and cling to trivial agendas and precedents, so they cannot deal with new developments creatively or efficiently. By contrast, the United States and Taiwan respond more swiftly to new situations because of flexibility on the part of their government officials.

A third factor is loss of self-confidence. Ever since 1985, with the rise of the bubble economy and its bursting, Japanese found that the methods they had relied on until then no longer worked, and this greatly eroded their confidence. If old methods produce only poor results, you ought to try new methods, but bureaucrats, politicians, and businesspeople either stick fast to doing things the way they have always done or give up trying to cope with the new situation at all. Nationalistic reactions have set in to fill the vacuum, as exemplified by the notion of the "Japan that can say no" to the United States.

Japan has accumulated enough economic and cultural strength to enable it to cope with new changes. It does not have to be so defensive. It can negotiate with Washington perfectly well without being extra-sensitive about its national pride and dignity.

Japanese seem to be living anxiously and hesitantly, conducting economic activities timidly. Whenever they meet Americans they posture and bluster in an effort to conceal their trepidation. They do not realize that Japan is not as weak as they might think.

They need to observe the United States with greater objectivity.

## Diversity Need Be Restored

Why, then, have Japanese lost their flexibility and become overly cautious? There are probably several reasons, but the loss of diversity in society seems to me to be the most responsible.

The source of vitality in any society is diversity and tolerance. The reason the United States can recover quickly each time it suffers difficulties is that it is a pluralistic society, has the capacity to accept diversity, and makes constant efforts to maintain those qualities. Taiwan's recent rapid growth is the result of our endeavor to build a tolerant society capable of making the most of diversity.

Japan today seems stuck with fixed ideas, as reflected in media reports and government policies. Its industrial policy lacks flexibility and diversity. Agricultural policy, for example, is so rigid that the government has done nothing for the nation's agriculture, which could be reinvigorated by, for example, introducing new farming units (other than the family) or encouraging incorporation among farmers. Japan should have a wider variety of agricultural policy options.

An expert in agricultural policy, I sometimes have the urge to take personal charge of farm policy, but for fear that it will become rigid, I refrain from doing so. Taiwan's agricultural future will come to a standstill unless those who think differently from the way I do and the younger generations are involved in considering, planning, and implementing agricultural policy from now on. My job, rather, is to open the path for them to display their abilities to the greatest advantage. This will encourage policy diversity.

Traditionally, Japan had a wealth of diversity and depth. Perhaps these have been pushed backstage because their significance is no longer appreciated. Vested interests also prevent the diverse and deeper elements of society from coming into full play.

## What Japan Can Do to Regain Its Strength

Japanese should remember that their country is by no means weak. It possesses tremendous strength. Economically, Toyota Motor and Honda Motor, for example, are vigorous. Matsushita Electric, too, it goes without saying, is robust, and Sony, despite recent reports of the red ink it chalked up due to exchange losses, is still a top-notch multinational corporation.

I would propose that Japanese stop dwelling on their shortcomings and take note of their strengths instead. If they put their heads together and list the positive elements of their country, they should come up with something like the following.

Possessing a culture of great diversity and depth is one of Japan's strongest points. It has accumulated a wealth of advanced technology in a wide spectrum of fields, and the population of 125 million shares this huge pool of technology. Japan is also the world's largest creditor nation, holding huge assets in the form of bonds, loans, and investments in the United States and other countries. It has extended overseas assistance of various kinds to other countries in Asia and elsewhere for many years and has cultivated considerable connections with them in the process.

Japanese industry is truly outstanding, led by a number of highly reputed, world-class companies. Even when the nation's economy is sluggish, many maintain excellent performance records and export high-quality products to world markets. There are still quite a few talented, energetic individuals of leadership caliber in Japan, although right now they are unable to put their potential to full use, hindered as they are by the intricate web of vested interests. If conditions change even a little, however, they will no doubt begin to play a major role in business and government.

Japanese now seem to have too little confidence in themselves to take advantage of the unusual and precious strengths they possess. They should take a cooler look around and reappraise themselves. This is what other Asian countries—what the world—wants them to do.

Even now I read a great deal, and most of the books I pick up tend to be Japanese because I am drawn to the depth of Japanese culture that is encapsulated in books. I also read many books from America, though not in the same numbers. The United States is a truly great country, and its greatness lies in its diversity and open-mindedness. Japan, too, is a great country, and its greatness is reflected in its profound culture accumulated over the centuries.

## Toward Greater Realism in International Politics

Now on the threshold of the twenty-first century, Japan should contribute internationally not only in the realm of the economy. Its role in world politics and security is also crucial. What Japan does is rapidly increasing in importance for Taiwan, too.

The problems Japan faces in the area of security are far more serious than Japanese people realize. What happened in 1995 is a case in point. That year, the U.S. Seventh Fleet aircraft carrier *Independence*, which had left Yokosuka port, arrived in Kyushu and asked for entry to refuel. Despite the terms of the U.S.–Japan security treaty, the Japanese government refused to grant the request. This came as a surprise to the world, but under Japanese law, emergency supply of fuel even to an ally is not permitted. It is my understanding, therefore, that Japan handed over some fuel to a foreign oil company which transported it in its own tanker to the *Independence*. Later, in April 1996, Japan and the United States concluded an acquisition and cross-servicing agreement (ACSA), which makes emergency fuel supply possible, but only in peacetime.

There are many in Japan who oppose the U.S.-Japan alliance. The Japan Communist Party, which has recently restored relations with the Chinese Communist Party, is expected to grow even more critical of the security arrangements. Some media organizations willingly carry articles calling for "review of the U.S.–Japan security arrangement."

However, American security studies expert Joseph Nye wrote in his well-known report that peace cannot be maintained in Asia unless one hundred thousand U.S. troops are permanently stationed in the region. U.S. Asia policy is unlikely to deviate much from that line.

From the standpoint of U.S. foreign policy today, however, it is difficult to build up a system of joint defense against potential enemies embracing the entirety of Asia. It would probably be impossible to forge an Asian version of the North Atlantic Treaty Organization (NATO) or Organization for Security and Cooperation in Europe (OSCE). A major reason is that the current U.S. policy of engagement toward the Chinese continent stresses and aims for incorporating the mainland, regardless of its political system, into the new international order. This policy line, however, is incompatible with the idea of a collective security system against common potential enemies. The United States is, therefore, forced to give up a comprehensive security system and form separate bilateral arrangements with Japan, the Republic of Korea, the Philippines, Indonesia, and Australia and to develop a security policy based on these separate treaties.

## Substantial Changes in the U.S.–Japan Security Treaty

During the Cold War era, in the guidelines for the U.S–Japan security treaty, the Soviet Union was seen as a potential enemy. The bilateral security system, therefore, was premised on this particular country. Then the Soviet Union collapsed.

Now, as efforts are being made to incorporate Russia into regional collective security, strained relations between Russia and mainland China are being eased. Feeling secure about Russia, the mainland will likely withdraw many troops from the north and transfer them to the south.

In the future there is a possibility that mainland China may be virtually contained in such areas as Central Asia, Siberia, the Korean Peninsula, and the Taiwan Strait. But this is impossible in the context of the current U.S. policy toward Peking. The

United States no doubt has think tanks and research institutes calling for containment of the Chinese continent by Russia, North and South Korea, Japan, Taiwan, and ASEAN. Such an idea will never see the light of day as long as the U.S. government advocates engagement with the PRC.

In the Japanese Diet, opposition party members question the prime minister and the Defense Agency director-general, asking if the new U.S.–Japan defense guideline is premised on the view of mainland China as a potential enemy. Answers like "realistically, one cannot tell what kind of an emergency will arise until it happens" are repeated over and over. The security issue in Japan, moreover, involves the question of revision of the Constitution, and any attempt to rescind the no-war provision of Article 9 arouses opposition not only within the country but from other Asian countries. If revision is indeed carried out, confusion will be unavoidable.

Rather than engaging in a constitutional debate, Japan should review the scope of cooperation it can extend to U.S. forces. To reach workable solutions at the working level of discussions, Japan's policy line should be based on an evaluation of realistic needs as well as past methods. Negotiations at that level may lead as far as consideration of the transportation capability of Japanese vessels and reciprocal identification of Taiwan's destroyers. Although these are not current problems, they may become issues in the future and should be considered in advance.

### Vision for Economic Cooperation in Asia
Security is an important challenge, of course, but Japan should

also play a more active role in the area of the economy. It should commit itself to an economic cooperation system for Asia. Recently the Japanese government has become more active via the concept of an Asia Monetary Fund (AMF) and the Miyazawa Plan, it is true, but the problem of adjusting conflicting interests with the United States remains.

I do not think Japan has to cling to the idea that it should try to do something independent of Washington on regional economic matters. It is advisable that Tokyo should take the initiative in an Asian economic cooperation system, involving itself in such a way that Washington cannot but approve and help the effort.

Take ASEAN, for example. It is not in a very favorable economic situation right now, but sooner or later ASEAN countries will once more sustain economic growth. When that happens, it is only Japan that will be able to keep the ASEAN members firmly together. So far, Japan has extended to these nations huge amounts in financial assistance, and many of its corporations have relocated production sites to the region. However, Japan's involvement is somewhat lacking in commitment, and for that reason it has yet to win the confidence of the host countries. These nations will not feel secure unless Japan becomes a politically more sophisticated actor in the region.

If Japan hesitates to take economic leadership in Asia, mainland China is likely to steal the limelight. Although this would by no means be welcomed by ASEAN, Peking may cut in and begin to dominate the regional scene.

Taiwan's desire to join ASEAN has been thwarted by opposition from the Peking regime. Considering Taiwan's geographic location and the economic role it plays, it is disadvantageous to both Taiwan and ASEAN for this situation to continue. Unfortunately the mainland's policy stands in the way.

In order to return the situation to normalcy, it is major powers like Japan, whose presence makes a difference, that should act. Japanese are not aware of the great hopes ASEAN countries place in them.

### A Larger Role in APEC

The same may be said of the larger-scale, Asia–Pacific regional forum, APEC. Among its members Taiwan participates as an economic entity. In other words, Taiwan in the capacity of an economic entity is a member equal in status with the other members. As usual, mainland China complains. I am aware that my participation in an APEC leaders' meeting would result in according Taiwan the same treatment as other nations both in name and fact, which would greatly irritate Peking. I therefore refrain from participating myself, but Taiwan is treated equally with other members in the committees under the APEC general assembly.

Oddly enough, APEC discussion does not deal with agriculture very much despite the fact that the economies of most of the ASEAN countries are agriculture-based. So at the APEC conference held in Indonesia, our representatives proposed a subcommittee to discuss agricultural problems. The United States could only agree to the proposal, and Taiwan chaired this meeting.

When the Asian currency crisis erupted in 1997, we talked about the necessity for a mutual-assistance system within ASEAN, a system in which a country in an economic crisis could issue national bonds which would be purchased by other ASEAN members. When we talked about that idea, our representatives proposed to Peking that Taiwan and the mainland work together in providing loans to ASEAN countries. Peking declined the proposal, saying that the mainland could not cooperate with the joint lending scheme because Taiwan was not a country. Despite these roadblocks by Peking, Taiwan takes every opportunity to offer proposals that will help ASEAN, and at the same time call attention to its own presence. Taiwan's endeavor in this area will be far more effective if Japan supports it. Japan's greater role will expand the options for ASEAN and APEC members.

## Politicians with Broad Outlooks Needed

Having learned a great deal from Japan first as a student and then in my career as an administrator, I find it hard to watch Japan in its present stalemate, unable to develop to its full potential. It also saddens me to see Japan act sometimes quite naively in the international arena. Among the factors responsible for Japan's sluggish response are what may be called its "inherent traits," in addition to its postwar experiences and the hereditary succession of politicians I mentioned earlier. Characteristically, Japanese can display their abilities to the full only when they serve a supporting role such as adviser or staff officer; but when they attempt to act as leader their weaknesses are suddenly revealed.

Whatever the situation, they are serious-minded and work very hard. It is this diligence that sustains their economic prosperity, and it is this seriousness that is reflected in their political behavior. No matter how fine the parts may be that were built with devotion and diligence, they will not work together nor be expected to function effectively as a whole if a certain factor is missing. This factor is not what Japanese people think of as "ability"; it is rather a sort of spiritual power, which could be called faith. Japanese seem to have only a small measure of this faith. Certainly they are lacking in self-confidence. That is why there seems to be little punch in whatever they do. They seem unable to take action with absolute confidence and conviction.

As far as Japanese politicians are concerned, it seems to me that, while adept at tending to parts and details, they are poor at grasping the whole picture from a broad viewpoint. As a result, they are always discussing stopgap measures. That proclivity reveals their lack of faith and self-confidence.

### Develop a Broad Perspective

As I see it, Japanese in general, not just politicians, have ceased to cultivate spiritual discipline. In terms of rationality and efficiency it may be sufficient only to develop "abilities," but human beings are not that simple.

As I mentioned in the first chapter, what I have learned most from Japanese thought is the importance of spiritual training. If one needs to develop a perspective that goes beyond rational, logical "ability" or ideas that transcend the calculation of self-interest, one must experience the state of mind where ability and interest are not the parameters of worth.

Training that is not directly oriented to the improvement of abilities and the promotion of interests is slighted today, but Japanese need now, more than ever, a perspective that is beyond such mundane considerations. Since Japanese tend to be somewhat overly concerned with details, this bias should be corrected by cultivating a broad perspective.

I would like to encourage our Japanese friends to revive their traditions of spiritual discipline, such as sitting in meditation at a *dojo* or getting up early in the morning to clean rooms and streets, something people do not ordinarily want to do.

Such training is exceedingly simple, but it is something that has all but disappeared in today's Japan. It is an element that I believe is not unrelated to what is missing in Japanese politics today. As long as politicians make judgments solely on the yardsticks of ability and interests and as long as people are educated in that direction, broad perspectives and new vision will not flourish in Japanese politics.

Suppose a person is eager to become prime minister, so he studies very hard, acquires everything considered necessary in the world of politics, and learns to understand economic issues. By earning the respect of the electorate he succeeds in his ultimate goal and attains the post of prime minister. Now, what will he do next? If his ultimate purpose was to capture the prime ministership, his goal has been fulfilled and he seeks nothing more. But this hardly makes sense. Such a politician, feeling at a loss for what to strive for next, will have confused the end and the means. If he asks himself what he wants to accomplish as prime minister, he will not know because he has never thought about it.

Japanese politics is overly well-mannered and obsessively attentive to minute detail. The same can be said of the process of climbing up the ladder of success in politics: it requires excessive concern with trivialities.

Politicians must take care to set aside their concern for ability and interests once in a while. This requires them to obtain a broad and comprehensive grasp of the issues, a necessary trait regardless of their abilities and interests. Some politicians not only have ability and are sensitive about conflicting interests but also can think broadly. Others do not have much ability and continue to pursue certain interests, but because they have a broad perspective they often are very successful as politicians. In any case, what is required of politicians is the willpower to think broadly, and to back up their thinking with commitment.

### Problem-solving with Conviction

Some Japanese may dismiss my recommendation of spiritual discipline as something they consider "outdated." As I see it, the tendency among Japanese today to think of faith and confidence as old-fashioned is what prevents the emergence of politicians of caliber. Even to me, Japan today looks extremely formal and rigid. I have many Japanese friends who are scholars. They are all diligent and serious, but they appear to study for the sake of studying. Even scholars need to look squarely at the actual conditions of society, recognize real problems clearly, and commit themselves to building a better Japan.

With commitment and faith, they should address the public and observe the realities of politics for themselves. When I was studying at Kyoto Imperial University and later, writing my dissertation at Cornell University, I not only worked hard but would always ask myself how my studies would benefit my fellow countrymen in Taiwan.

I am certainly not the only one who has had such thoughts. In Japan as well, right after the Meiji Restoration of 1868, students and politicians were committed to making their country better, and their determination became especially strong when they toured and studied abroad. The same commitment was felt by Japanese who found themselves in a foreign land thinking of their fellow countrymen in the early postwar period.

What matters most is faith, or commitment, as well as self-confidence and discipline. I am reminded of their importance each time I observe the political confusion in today's Japan and whenever I hear about the various areas of Japanese society that suffer from stagnation or gridlock.

# CHAPTER 6

# A Trilateral Effort in Asia

$A$s ASIA enters the twenty-first century, one factor that is going to loom large in the region is Taiwan's relations with the United States, on the one hand, and with Japan, on the other. The kind of relationships we build are going to have as big an impact politically as they do economically.

## Taiwan's Relations with the United States and Japan

Right now, the importance of the relations between Taiwan and Japan tends to be downplayed in the absence of formal diplomatic relations and government-level ties between them. In the case of the United States, however, even though there are no formal diplomatic relations, a well-developed network of exchange and contacts with Taiwan has taken shape. No matter how their relationships stand in diplomatic terms, however, the fact remains that Taiwan, the United States, and Japan are closely bound in a complementary relationship that can only grow stronger with time.

To begin with, they are bound together for economic reasons in a delicate triangular relationship. Taiwan imports an enormous volume of goods from Japan. In 1998 the total value of imports from Japan was more than US$27 billion. While exports from Taiwan to Japan in the same year were considerably lower, totaling US$9.3 billion and leaving Taiwan with a trade deficit of US$17.7 billion, the greater part of the imports comprises vitally important plant and equipment, parts, and raw materials. Besides differences in the level of technology between Taiwan and Japan, other factors in the trade imbalance include the falling yen and the slump in Japan's semiconductor industry, which reduced the volume of imports from Taiwan. These trends only underscore the need to push technological development in Taiwan and expand the Japanese market.

Taiwan enjoys an export surplus in its bilateral trade across the Pacific, but even though the United States continues to provide a huge market, Taiwan's surplus has shrunk considerably in the past decade. The main factor in the decline has been the rising tide of investment in the Chinese mainland by Taiwanese enterprises, and with it a change in the pattern of exports: as more goods are exported by way of mainland China, the volume of direct exports from Taiwan decreases. What is important here, however, is that Taiwan also has a trade surplus with the mainland, and so it uses the earnings from its exports to the Chinese mainland and the United States to pay for imports from Japan.

Until very recently Asia's economies appeared poised to take off like a flock of geese, soaring into the future with Japan in the lead and the others following in regular formation. It was the American market the formation was aimed at.

Unfortunately, Asia's economic surge had been premised on an economic order that collapsed before it could take solid shape. First came the rapid appreciation of the yen following the 1985 Plaza Accord, and then in 1994 mainland China devalued the renminbi. With the rise in the value of the dollar, the Asian economies, pegged to the dollar at that time, started to sink into financial crisis.

In July 1997 Thailand cut the baht loose from the dollar, setting off a chain reaction that hit the Philippines, Malaysia, Indonesia, and Hong Kong, wreaking financial havoc. In rapid succession exchange rates plummeted in all those countries except Hong Kong, and their economies were left mired in inflation, rising unemployment, and double-digit negative growth rates.

The financial crisis that swept through East Asia can be attributed to the following five factors: (1) investment levels consistently outpaced domestic savings; (2) the inflow of short-term foreign capital disguised deficits in the current balance; (3) the allocation of domestic investment was not necessarily rational or economically sound; (4) pegging national currencies to the dollar over the long term had the effect of decimating their competitive power internationally; and (5) these countries rushed too precipitously to liberalize and internationalize credit, and they were unable to adopt appropriate financial measures in the process. Taken together, those developments were directly responsible for the financial crisis in East Asia.

Taiwan switched to a floating exchange rate in 1990, and today its foreign reserves surpass US$90 billion, up dramatically from the 1985 level of US$25 billion. In 1985 Taiwan's per capita national income was slightly over US$3,000; currently that figure stands at roughly US$13,000.

Nonetheless, the generally rising dollar and falling yen during the past few years are having a negative effect on Taiwan's economy. The yen need not rise too high, as it once did, but it has to be kept strong enough to reflect Japan's economic fundamentals and to help Asian economies recover.

## Managing the Financial System

Our uneasiness stems from the persistent, long-unresolved headache of Japan's bad bank loans and continuing rapid fluctuations in the region's exchange rates. Again, from the Taiwanese standpoint, we would like to see these problems settled as soon as possible and international economic order restored.

In the case of Taiwan, it was mostly credit unions that were threatened by bad debts, but before real trouble could occur the government stepped in to contain the damage by encouraging mergers. Also, beginning in about 1990, the government began prodding banks to raise the level of their capital adequacy, with the result that today they all surpass the minimum Bank for International Settlements requirement of 8 percent. Improved capital adequacy ratios helped to prevent overlending and kept Taiwan's banking institutions on a solid footing.

Even then, it was estimated that a considerable volume of bad bank loans would remain at the end of April 1999, and for that reason the Ministry of Finance announced on February 19 the adoption of several measures aimed at clearing away the bad loans as quickly as possible. First, the business tax paid by banks would be cut from 5 percent to 3 percent. Second, the Central Bank cut the bank reserve rate from 7.65 percent to 6.41 percent, thereby releasing NT$166.8 billion back into the banking system. These measures ought to enable Taiwan's banks to wipe the slate clean on their bad loans within four years. We can also expect the sluggish stock market to rebound quickly and with vigor.

One problem in Taiwan is the credit bureaus of agricultural

associations, which are similar to the financial institutions run by the agricultural cooperatives in Japan. In Taiwan's case, they are not incorporated as joint stock corporations, and consequently they are run with almost no capital of their own. Since this setup for credit unions is extremely risky, they will have to be duly incorporated and adequate measures devised to increase their net worth.

The bedrock of Taiwan's economy is small- and medium-sized industries, which account for 98 percent of all industry in Taiwan. In order to help them obtain capital and create business opportunities, the government has set up a capital fund for developing small businesses and another fund that guarantees their access to credit.

The biggest threat to Taiwan's economic health right now, as with other countries in the region, is the rapidly fluctuating exchange rate. During 1998–99 alone the shifting exchange rate has cut Taiwan's currency value by 20 percent, which, calculated in dollars, has effectively eroded 20 percent of Taiwan's export value in that period.

I tell the people of Taiwan that, "The money in your pocket will stay the same. Exports may have decreased by 20 percent, but since the rate of exchange is also 20 percent lower, your export earnings in Taiwan's currency hasn't changed. We're giving plenty of thought to these issues, too." Irrespective of this as the lower exchange rate has the effect of reducing our foreign reserves in the long run, we are anxious that this situation not drag on.

Several years ago I had a meeting with top officials of the Central Bank of Taiwan and other government officials in charge of fiscal policy to talk about Taiwan's current political and economic situation, taking Hidaka Yoshiki's "Washington Secretary Report" as our point of departure. The substance of Hidaka's report, which forecast the international economic situation, came very close to our own analysis.

My main concern, however, focused on something slightly different. Addressing the group, I said:

> I called you here today to hear your opinions about the "Washington Secretary Report," but what I really want to talk about is Taiwan. Given the trends outlined in the report, what is going to be most important for Taiwan?
>
> I don't have to be a financial expert to know that the rapid changes taking place in international finance are clearly having a huge economic and political impact. It would be suicidal to ignore them in managing our financial system.
>
> Money is no longer just a 'bearer of value' or a shadow of the real economy that it once was, as economists used to argue. Monetary policy cannot just consider issues of money supply. Today, money itself can be traded like a kind of goods. We have seen money become the object of such active speculation that financial transactions now move the whole economy.

Since a national currency can be bought and sold in futures transactions, the consequent rise and fall of its value affects the economic fortunes of the nation itself. The amount of money involved in a single day of business in the foreign exchange markets of the world far exceeds one trillion dollars. That is thirty-four times the volume of transactions conducted in goods and services.

This is the environment in which foreign money, in the form of short-term capital for purposes of speculation, is now being brought into Taiwan. Such speculation going on amid the radically changing and highly competitive international environment makes it all the more imperative that Taiwan upgrade its industrial production and keep employment strong, while expanding its exports and imports.

In his book *The Crisis of Global Capitalism*, American financier George Soros makes it very clear how imperfect the market is. According to him, the financial market today is not just a passive reflection of what is happening in the real economy. It is actively shaping the real economy. There are times when financial markets supply plenty of capital—more than necessary—for the real economy, and other times when they provide only a trickle. The reach of that ebb and flow has a palpable effect on the real economy, which is why there is a great deal of risk involved in the excessive expansion of financial markets.

The danger is that financial markets are easily destabilized, and so if they become too strong a force, they could destroy the very foundations of the free market. As long as we depend on the market economy, we are going to need some kind of regulations for the maintenance of market stability.

## Interconnectedness in Asia

What happens to the renminbi (Rmb) in mainland China is going to be a problem from now on. The PRC has an agreement with the United States promising not to devalue its currency, but it is far from certain that the mainland economy can really sustain itself and keep the renminbi at its present level. Bad bank loans amount to 20 percent of the gross national product, and industries have unsold inventory totaling about Rmb250 billion in value, according to *The Washington Post*.

Taiwan needs to map out carefully considered measures to deal with this situation. If the renminbi is devalued, Taiwan's exports to mainland China will necessarily decrease. Whenever the currency of a country falls in value, the volume of imports decreases as a matter of course. Nevertheless, to hold the renminbi steady at its current level is going to create pressures on the economy of mainland China.

In fact, problems have already begun to appear. Taiwanese businesses have invested in as many as 30,000 enterprises in mainland China, and right now they are experiencing two kinds of dilemmas. One is that payments due on goods sold are not coming in as they should, which makes it extremely difficult to obtain sufficient operating funds. The other is that these firms have to turn out products in order to make money, so they continue to manufacture. But their goods are not selling and their inventories are growing.

Taiwanese businesses that invested in Indonesia, on the other hand, are making large profits. Some shoemaking firms and plastic manufacturers, for example, are seeing their profits triple. What has allowed them to do so well is the currency depreciation in Indonesia, which has brought down the labor costs of production. Calculated in dollars, wages in that country have fallen to less than one-third the wage level in mainland China.

Such a situation lays open the possibility for economic imbalances and friction to arise within Asia. Taiwan needs to be very cautious in its relations with other countries to prevent its own commercial enterprises from being swamped in acrimony. In Indonesia, for example, local people have formed a private policing unit that protects Taiwan's companies. For their part, the companies, which are making even more money than before, pay gratuities to members of the policing unit for the protection.

Japan's economic recovery is a critical factor in rebuilding Asia. For almost a decade, ever since the bubble burst, Japan has had trouble trying to pull out of the recession and get its economy back on a solid footing. Recently we have seen the yen growing stronger as government policies take effect, but the Japanese market keeps on shrinking; for Asian countries striving for stability through their export-oriented approach, Japan's market is no longer of much help.

We have to realize, therefore, how vital the United States has become as a market for Japanese and other Asian exports. The American market, in fact, offers Asia the only ray of hope for economic growth. But if, as is very possible, Asian exports to America undergo a rapid increase in the future, that in turn could provoke trade friction. However large a market the United States offers to the rest of Asia, it will take a stronger stance vis-à-vis Japan. Japan must act quickly to clear up its bad bank loans, adopt comprehensive measures to revive its stagnant economy, and at the same time keep the other Asian countries from getting trapped in a vicious circle of economic woes.

## Accurate Information on Asia

By now economic disparities have spread quickly throughout Asia, but the quality of reporting on actual conditions is abysmal, making it exceedingly difficult to get full, accurate information. What information is produced, and this by people there on the spot, is filled with errors, discrepancies, and omissions.

Take a recent example in Hong Kong. A while ago talk went around that quite a few people in the Hong Kong branches of Japan's trading houses were being demoted. Of course no one would actually use the word "demotion," but to be relieved of one's duties in Hong Kong and sent home amounted to the same thing, it appeared.

As to why this was happening, the reports and other information sent from Hong Kong to the head offices were often unreliable and wrong. When it receives so much misinformation, a head office has a hard time formulating a workable strategy for the company. Most observers tend to underestimate the scope of changes taking place in Hong Kong. Except for a small number of people, not even Taiwanese or Americans truly grasp what is happening in Hong Kong.

They don't seem to realize that if they want sufficient and accurate information about a place like that, they are going to have to probe, dig, study, and think. In Hong Kong's case, one must factor in not only the economic bias but also political and social biases woven into local accounts.

It is rumored that there was a tacit agreement made at the wish of the Japanese consulate, JETRO, and the Japanese government itself to give an optimistic tone to information, to the effect that "prospects are good." Thinking short term, they probably believed that a positive picture would not create problems, but in the long term business cannot shape effective responses when the actual situation is not made clear.

The same is true in Singapore. Conditions in Singapore are far more serious than is routinely reported in Japan, Taiwan, and other countries. The economy is burdened with an unexpectedly large volume of debt, which has brought a good many businesses to financial impasse.

I have no wish to denigrate other Asian countries by pointing out these examples. My concern is rather that Taiwan, the United States, and Japan should fully engage with Asia, and that will be possible only if they have consistently realistic and accurate information. Without such information, no one can write the prescription that will bring Asia's economy back to good health, and if they try and prescribe the wrong medicine, the disease will only get worse.

Even though much effort is being made to revitalize the ailing economies of Asian countries, neither individual investors nor corporations have an accurate, unbiased picture of what is really happening on the ground. Of the several factors that frustrate attempts to get a clear picture, one is a lack of transparency in these countries and areas that obscure what is going on and how economic activities are being carried out. Let's say you are thinking about making a substantial investment; you soon discover that it is next to impossible to find out about the solvency of the prospective enterprise. It is as though there were no such thing as reliable accounting systems or auditing procedures.

Another factor is political. The financial crisis has gone deep enough now to affect the real economy itself, which means that attempts to accelerate recovery are going to involve some major, systemic adjustments. Such adjustments entail costs, and the burden of the costs must necessarily be spread out. But who shares the burden and how much is the load? Those decisions are by nature political. Certain problems require political solutions, like banks with bad credit, bureaucracies that have made policy blunders, and government officials or their families involved in corruption and embezzlement. Until such situations are improved, investors and foreign aid donors are going to think twice before committing any money.

There are information problems with North Korea as well. The information that reaches Japan is perhaps not completely false, but much of it is piecemeal and fragmentary. Given my position as a third party, I cannot make any definitive statements, but it seems to me that the only way we can understand how North Korea ended up in its present state is by looking at it in terms of the geopolitical structure of Asia as a whole.

In August 1998 North Korea sent a missile right into Japan's territorial waters, leaving everyone anxious and puzzled. Then it was reported that an underground nuclear processing facility had been identified by an American reconnaissance satellite. It is crucial that we carefully analyze the North Korean intentions behind these reckless actions, actions that are going to have an impact on the unification of the Korean peninsula. Certainly the United States may have to reassess its policy of engagement vis-à-vis North Korea.

The United States is far better informed about actual conditions in North Korea today than is Japan; hence, the United States is working on settling problems with a minimum of repercussions in surrounding areas. In the long run, however, interference by the Communist Party of mainland China may prevent North Korea from seeking a new approach for itself.

We do not have formal diplomatic relations with North Korea on the state level, but we definitely do not disregard that country. The problems of North Korea concern all of Asia. The world needs an accurate understanding of what is really going on there, and for that it is essential to have solid, reliable information.

Has the famine, for example, really become as dire as many reports say? It is difficult to respond to such a situation when there is no way of knowing for sure how serious it is. Again, valid information on the technology used in building the missile that North Korea sent over Japan could be extremely important: Where did it come from? What level of technology was it?

It is also not widely known that Washington promised aid to Pyongyang and then put it on hold when confronted by intense lobbying in the U.S. Congress by South Korean politicians. There was even talk of Russia taking over the aid project.

In Japan, the only issue that has received sustained and focused attention is the series of abductions of Japanese to North Korea. These have been reported for humanitarian reasons, but unless Japanese can comprehend the broad circumstances at work in North Korea, they won't be able to move forward in solving that problem, either. Meanwhile, a certain Asian politician is said to have wisely advised the Pyongyang government that if the abduction problem could be settled, North Korea would gain a much better standing in Asia. Yet Japan still finds it impossible to detect, much less make use of, the hidden activities going on below the surface.

## A Regional System of Financing

When the currency crisis hit Asia, Japan pushed for the establishment of an Asian version of the IMF, the Asian Monetary Fund (AMF), but the United States was against it. Later, when Japan proposed a system of regional aid to be administered within Asia, which came to be known as the Miyazawa Plan, the Americans were amenable. However, Europe was reluctant, worried about the economic frictions that may be created by a yen-based plan for financing to help stabilize Asia's economies.

Meanwhile, another assistance program that would be run through the Asian Development Bank (ADB) has already won the support of the majority of APEC members. According to the plan, a country in need of capital issues bonds guaranteed by its own government, and these are then sold by the ADB to Japan, Taiwan, or any country whose economy is comparatively stable.

Since the program allows no preference for any particular national currency and the United States and other leading economies have raised little objection, this method of obtaining capital assistance appears to be very promising. Until now Taiwan, for its part, has been purchasing as many ADB bonds as it can.

This approach to financing would seem especially advantageous to Malaysia. If Malaysia can build up its economic base sufficiently and if it were to issue bonds through the ADB, Taiwan and probably other countries as well would gladly buy them. A proposal to this effect was actually submitted to the board of directors at the ADB, but little has yet been done about it so far.

Compared with the AMF idea or the Miyazawa Plan, using the ADB seems to me to be more realistic and to have a far greater chance of succeeding. Like it or not, in the "new international order" now being molded by the United States, any emerging system that Americans cannot control may not be very welcome. Asia needs to build an effective system to resolve the regional financial crisis, but it must be done without creating serious friction.

In Japan, on the other hand, discussions of the Asian economy tend toward the facile contention that "Europe did it; why can't we?" Japanese reason that if Europe could switch to a single currency, which it did in 1999, then, theoretically at least, Asia could do the same thing.

Hopes were high as plans for a unified European currency progressed, and there is undeniable historical significance in this emerging economic unity among countries that were, within living memory, engaged in terrible, protracted warfare. But there are still many problems.

First of all, it is not certain how well the "euro fund" will succeed in attracting money from around the world. Also, England has yet to join, and the rivalry between Germany and France has by no means disappeared. I think we can expect political discord to continue for some time.

Among other economic problems are major differences in industrial structure and large disparities in productivity among member countries. If they want to succeed in the goal of economic integration, moreover, all the members are going to have to endure constraints on their fiscal policy.

In one respect the euro-currency countries are already united; their desire for economic unity stems from a shared antipathy to having to constantly follow the American lead. On that point even Germany and France find common ground for compromise and cooperation. Nonetheless, with so many issues to resolve, the near future for Europe does not promise smooth sailing.

The idea that Asia ought to have a unified currency like the euro should not be lightly advocated. When I was interviewed by the Japanese writer Fukada Yusuke for the monthly opinion journal *Shokun*, I talked about the difficult position of Asia, wedged between the two major currencies, the dollar and the euro, and possible ways to deal with the situation. In my way of thinking, I said, we face the same problem as that posed by the security issue; Japan has to become more actively involved with ASEAN before we can even begin to consider the possibility of a unified Asian currency. First, we need to establish some system to ensure stability in the exchange rate and to sustain real economic growth. What is crucial is that the system not devolve into an exclusive bloc pitted against the dollar and the dollar sphere.

Such a system is only possible when all of us, the United States, Japan, mainland China, Taiwan, Singapore, and every other country involved, take a little more responsibility and more active initiative in running APEC. It seems to me that we have focused too narrowly on free trade; we have forgotten about the financial crisis in Asia and the problems of agriculture, a vitally important and neglected sector.

Let us think globally and reconsider the Bretton Woods system centering on the IMF and the World Bank. This system, in which the U.S. dollar is the core currency, seems no longer able to maintain stability in the international monetary system. Presently, the world is awash in paper money and everywhere you look someone is acquiring someone else's assets. This is where the United States can propose measures to help establish the financial policies and facilities necessary to ensure stability in the world economy.

We also hope that Japan, for its part, will consider using Overseas Development Assistance (ODA) to furnish long-term capital loans to Asian countries. We should aim at building a system that assures optimal allocation of capital, thereby enabling recipient countries to start accumulating capital.

### Choose Taiwan

Nowadays the first choice for an investor with some extra money is to buy American corporate stock, and the second, the euro fund. Japanese and American investors are no exception. But are those really the best places to put their money? I propose they choose Taiwan.

Taiwan presently has a number of large national projects under way, one of which is a high-speed railway like Japan's bullet train. Corporate delegations from several countries in Europe have been to Taiwan for discussions about assistance in technology and financing costs, but there has been no clear proposal from Japan.

I would like to see more large-scale American and Japanese investments in Taiwan. Taiwan is a reliable investment target; its economy has ample room for growth and it has stability economically and socially.

It is disappointing, therefore, that while Germany is interested enough in the high-speed rail system to send top-level government officials to Taiwan to continue talks, negotiations with Japan have not progressed beyond basic items, which are: (1) bidding price, (2) safety, and (3) political considerations. Political considerations refers to the fact that money going into this project has to come from private sources, but we would like the Japanese government to give some indication of its support for the project.

Taiwan's economic ties with the United States and Japan are already extensive. It continues to have a US$17 billion trade deficit with Japan, but if Japanese companies were to manufacture more in Taiwan, as we have been encouraging them to do, that would take care of the deficit.

Japanese investors have built factories in Taiwan to produce such goods as picture tubes for TVs, computer monitors, compressors for air conditioners, and controllers for robots. Taiwan should also be working on arrangements for the domestic manufacture of products that are being imported. And since Taiwan depends on the U.S. for many items used in advanced technology, it would be beneficial to Taiwan if Taiwanese living in the United States were to develop technology and invest in manufacturing projects together with American partners.

Taiwan is now the world's largest producer of cathode-ray picture tubes, and it has the technology to make other such products. But in some areas its level of technology is still inadequate. Therefore, Taiwan hopes that foreign (especially Japanese and American) corporations will build factories in Taiwan to make technology transfer possible for domestic manufacture of goods in those fields.

All three countries would gain from active American and Japanese investment growing hand in hand with technological development in Taiwan. At the same time, they would forge closer and deeper relationships.

## Specter of Hegemony

Closer relations between Taiwan and the United States and between Taiwan and Japan would bring numerous advantages, in both the economic and political realms. As I have repeatedly stressed, Taiwan has a future only if it exists, and Asia's future is tied to the continued existence of Taiwan. One could say that as long as Taiwan exists, its future will blossom, and its presence will help secure the future of Asia.

Taiwan's present status may well be defined as the Republic of China on Taiwan; it expresses our national identity and asserts our sovereignty and independence as a state. Some people in Taiwan would like to call it the Republic of Taiwan, but I do not think it would be right, nor is there a need for it.

To secure the unmistakable existence of Taiwan in the future, it is not enough just to reject easy assumptions about its status.

The entity of the Republic of China must also be firmly established on the basis of solid legal tenets. Before I finish my term as president, I intend to consult specialists in international law from many nations to determine a clearer definition of our sovereignty.

As long as mainland China maintains its hegemonic stance, peace will probably not come to Asia. The idea of a hegemonic, nationalistic "Greater China" is unquestionably a threat to mainland China's neighbors. Russia probably feels no pressure, but India is always on guard, determined to hold its own against Communist China. Other countries in the region are also made uneasy by a sense of threat from PRC borders. This is not the kind of environment where stability takes root.

It is regrettable that the country that appears to be the most timid on this point is Japan. Japanese always have an ear open to Peking in whatever they do, whether in their political activities or even in making interpretations of history.

Taiwan has its own identity as Taiwan, Tibet as Tibet, Xinjiang as Xinjiang, Inner Mongolia as Inner Mongolia, and the Tungpei as the Tungpei. Ideally, if each one were allowed to affirm its own existence, we would see Asia's regional stability enhanced. For purposes of effective management alone, "Greater China" would be better off divided into perhaps seven autonomous regions, which could then compete among themselves and with the world for progress.

But no such decentralization of power is likely to come about soon. That will not happen until Peking recognizes the autonomy and unique culture of each of these regions and gives them due respect.

Democratization in Taiwan has moved very rapidly over the last ten years. The political system originally designed to cope with the civil war between the Chinese Communist Party (CCP) and the Nationalist Party (KMT) has been dismantled. We have created a framework for our government based on the will of the people of Taiwan as expressed in free and·fair elections. Those achievements were hard-won through drastic reforms that built a free and just society and a democratic system. Determined to preserve for the future all that has been accomplished, Taiwan will never stop working to secure peace in the Taiwan Strait, for it is peace on which the future depends.

Taiwan's people and government together worked unremittingly to bring about the transformation of its politics and society—a process in which the Chinese mainland did not participate at all. And yet the mainland clings to the civil war mentality of the pre-democratic reform era, continuing to dangle the possibility that it might take unilateral military action against Taiwan. As far as Taiwan is concerned, civil war is a thing of the past. Taiwan faces mainland China in a relationship that transcends the "internal affairs of China" thesis, placing two political entities on a de facto equal footing.

Both the sea and air corridors of the Taiwan Strait, located in the western Pacific Ocean, are absolutely vital to international commercial shipping. The peace and security of the Strait are therefore "public assets" of the international community. Astonishingly, some American and Japanese Asia scholars and experts in strategy use purposely vague expressions, such as "The problem of Taiwan is the problem of the Chinese people," in effect endorsing mainland China's position on the peace and security of the Taiwan Strait.

Such fuzzy pronouncements amount to the relinquishment of control by the United States and Japan over their own vital interests. Taken to the extreme, this kind of thinking gets dangerously close to being trapped by Peking's ploys to weaken the United States and Japan while contriving to take over leadership in Asia. If Washington and Tokyo make any concession on this issue, the Chinese mainland will interpret it as waning concern with the Taiwan Strait, in turn encouraging Peking's impulse to hold military exercises of the type we saw in 1995-96.

## Japan's Failure to See the United States Objectively

Geographically, Japan is part of Asia, but politically, it is fully incorporated into the American strategy for the region. Since the collapse of the Soviet Union, furthermore, U.S. Asia strategy has stretched to cover a huge area that extends to the Middle East, and it is in that expanded frame that Japan is now placed. Consequently, the Japan-U.S. security treaty has been redefined: from an alliance formed as a defense against the communist bloc, it has turned into a treaty to monitor peace in Asia as a whole.

The document drafted by strategic affairs expert Joseph Nye, known as the Nye Report, which forms the basis for America's strategy in Asia, also places Japan within the larger context. Certainly, U.S. thinking now runs along such lines. But that is only the way the present American government sees Japan; it is up to Japan to be more positive in asserting its own stand in the interests of prosperity and peace in Asia.

Insofar as the American government, caught up in its "engagement" with mainland China, is unable to actually implement its strategies in the overall interest of Asia, relations among the separate countries in the region are beginning to take on more weight.

I would urge Japan to study more and work harder to learn about the United States. For fifty years Japan has gone along with and accommodated itself to American policy. After all this time, Japanese think they know more about the United States than any other country, but in my opinion that is a total misconception. In fact, in trailing in the footsteps of the United States, Japan has lost the ability to see that country with objectivity. At the same time, Japan seems to have become almost unconcerned about how to get across to the United States what it itself is thinking.

If there are no special channels or measures for either America or Japan to gain an understanding of the other, the only way both societies can learn about one another is to accept what comes through the mass media. Yet media reporting on "American intentions" or "Japanese thinking" contains very little that is accurate. I dwell on this point because it is not just Japan but all of Asia that will suffer the disturbing consequences if Japanese leaders are unable to truly understand American foreign policy objectives and cannot communicate their own country's intent to Americans.

## Drawing Mainland China into the World

I, too, am constantly gathering information to help me understand American thinking, and I use a variety of means to convey to Americans what Taiwan wants. Recently I was quite frank with one high-ranking American official when I told him, "This idea of 'engagement' with the mainland that you are talking about is flawed. What you need is not to be drawn closer to mainland China, but to draw the mainland out into the world."

As for the mainland leadership, undoubtedly they see very clearly how Mikhail Gorbachev's policies a decade ago helped to bring about the demise of the Soviet Union. It would be naive to think that they would let their country be enticed by some idea of "engagement" and walk out defenseless onto the international political stage. I do not think any of mainland China's leaders will ever forget the lesson of Gorbachev and the former Soviet Union.

Yet for Asia to enjoy long-term security without being threatened by a hegemonic great power, the only way is to draw mainland China out and integrate it into the world. Unless mainland China can manage its political life and economic affairs along lines that tally with what is acceptable in today's world, there is no hope. It is the crucial challenge, therefore, not just to Asia but to the world, that the hegemonic disposition of mainland China and problems inherent in its political and economic structures be replaced by cooperative, modern systems.

The United States is pushing its present strategic partnership with Peking as a useful approach on two points. First, maintaining a dialogue of a strategic nature, Washington hopes that visits back and forth by top government officials, military experts, and high-ranking military officers from both sides will serve to deepen mutual understanding. Second, the U.S. approach is to consider Peking not as an enemy but with goodwill. Differences that arise by virtue of conflicting positions could, in this way of thinking, be skirted for the sake of greater mutual gain.

This American "engagement" approach to mainland China, however, has some strategic defects. Knowing full well what American national interests are, Peking authorities are absolutely opposed to falling in line with current global standards of politics and economic practices. They feel compelled to demonstrate to the United States, Japan, and the rest of the world that mainland China is indeed a great power, which alone gives it the right to demand that the rules of international society be changed.

Communist China is fully aware of the contradictions that riddle its social system, but it will absolutely not put it own survival at risk through the political liberalization and democratization that Washington's "engagement" would entail. That is why mainland China has been so vociferous lately in its nationalist slogans, and so determined to strike back by putting pressure on the business world at home and abroad. Peking has been especially adamant in demanding that Washington accept mainland China's claims on the issue of Taiwan.

It is only natural that Taiwan should be the one most seriously concerned that the mainland makes changes in these areas. For one thing, Taiwan hopes that one day its own people together with their cousins on the mainland will enjoy the highest level of freedom and democracy. Just as important, Taiwan is eager to see the end of the threat from the Chinese mainland.

I want our American and Japanese friends to understand that this is not just Taiwan's problem. Taiwan's existence is important to Communist China and the world. If Taiwan can create and maintain an affluent, peaceful society, the mainland will be unable to sustain the current status quo and China as a whole will move toward the Taiwan model. But if Taiwan is swallowed up and controlled by Peking, the whole of China will fall under a hegemonic system, becoming a major threat to the world.

In case that should happen, furthermore, Japan will be next to face a mortal threat. Its geographic position is such that if Taiwan and the areas nearby were eclipsed and the sea lanes were cut off in the crisis, Japan would be isolated economically and militarily. However, very few Japanese fully appreciate how strategically important Taiwan is for their country. Taiwan is not just another island located somewhere to the south that happens to import a lot of Japanese high-tech goods; for Japan it is literally a lifeline.

# CHAPTER **7**

# Taiwan in the
# Twenty-first Century

$F$OR AT least two reasons, the Taipei city mayoral election of December 5, 1998 was a cause for celebration among the ruling KMT. First, the KMT candidate Ma Ying-jeou won, securing the office of mayor of Taipei, and second, more importantly, he won on the party's campaign theme of the "new Taiwanese." Let me explain.

### The New Taiwan, the New Taiwanese
Ma Ying-jeou's father was a member of the social elite who came to Taiwan from the Chinese mainland after 1949 and was therefore not an "early settler" Taiwanese. It was all the more significant, then, his father being a "latecomer" mainlander that Ma Ying-jeou could gather support and win with his campaign promise to take the country forward as a society of "new Taiwanese."

Running against Ma was the incumbent mayor, Democratic Progressive Party (DPP) candidate Chen Shui-bian, who called for independence with the campaign slogan "priority to Taiwan." Like myself, Chen is identified with the Taiwanese, and therefore his appeal to make Taiwan the central focus was persuasive. I advised Ma that if Chen were going to stress "priority to Taiwan," Ma should appeal to the electorate with the theme "Taiwan first." But voters needed to know what was meant by "Taiwan first."

When I ran for the presidency in 1996, my strongest showing was in districts with large numbers of Taiwanese voters, while Ma, with his mainlander father, could not rally those constituencies as easily. Yet he had to be able to swing the voters in the predominantly Taiwanese districts in order to win. If he could get strong support from those voters, his election was assured.

Hence, Ma dispelled the rivalry between the Taiwanese and mainlanders by issuing an appeal to rise above the discord and managed to gain the needed margin for victory in a very close race. His tactic began to take shape during a campaign speech I made, in which I suddenly confronted him with a question: "Listen, my friend Ma, where are you from? What *are you*?" With great dignity, Ma, facing the audience, rose and answered, "I was brought up in Taiwan and raised on the nourishing food of Taiwan. I love Taiwan. I am a new Taiwanese."

There was a roar of applause from the audience. With that, the campaign took off, propelled by an idea that immediately struck a chord among voters, Taiwanese and mainlanders alike— the idea of the "new Taiwanese."

Helped by the force of this appeal, Ma's victory was a sign that the people of Taiwan were finally moving in the direction that I had long hoped they would. The image of the KMT as the party brought over from the mainland, a party of "outsiders," is long out of date now. The effect of "new Taiwanese" is to confirm Taiwan's identity; the term sums up the achievement of the Taiwanese people in having created their own government and having established a political system that works for them. It reminds us all that the people of Taiwan are committed to building a flourishing and unbiased society.

We must not allow the KMT to retain even a vestige of the image as essentially an outside party brought in from mainland China. On October 24, 1998, the day before Retrocession Day (commemorating the reversion of Taiwan to the Republic of

China), I made a speech in which I said,

> All of us who grow and live on this soil today are Taiwanese
> people, whether we be aborigines or descendants of the abori-
> gines or descendants of the immigrants from the mainland who
> came over centuries or decades ago. We all have made
> equal contributions to Taiwan's development in the past, and
> share a common responsibility for Taiwan's future. It is a non-
> transferable duty for each one of us, the "new Taiwanese
> people," to convert our love and affection for Taiwan into con-
> crete actions in order to open up a grander horizon for its
> development. It is also our responsibility to establish a magnifi-
> cent vista for our descendants.

It was probably inevitable that in my time people distin-
guished between Taiwanese and mainlanders even in elections.
When I ran for the presidency in 1996 I certainly benefited from
votes gained in areas where Taiwanese were numerous. But
henceforth politicians and politics must move on in the debate,
leaving the old distinctions behind and making the identity of
"new Taiwanese" the new point of departure.

## Taiwan in History
Taiwan's original settlers were a group of relatively small but
culturally diverse tribes. The first Westerners to attempt to gain
control of the island were the Dutch, who came in the seventeenth century, soon after Han Chinese, mostly from Fukien and
Kwangtung provinces, began coming over from the mainland.

Migration from the mainland is thought to have increased
exponentially during the Ch'ing dynasty, bringing the popula-

tion of Han Chinese from a hundred and some thousand in the seventeenth century to well over two million by the end of the era. The Japanese occupation began in 1895, and in 1949 the KMT entered Taiwan en masse. Thus the island embraced a broad range of peoples and cultures at that time, and now, fifty years later, it has become the home of the "new Taiwanese."

This fabric of history becomes more relevant when we consider Taiwan in the twenty-first century. The reality and significance of Taiwan's existence today is that of a civilized state, absorbing diverse cultures from outside and embracing people of many ethnic origins as it builds its future.

Rather than culling and rejecting, the process of growth should add to and enrich what we already have. Taiwan exists today precisely because of the meritorious efforts of our forebears. The "new Taiwanese" did not come out of nowhere. They are a creation of the many layers our history has accumulated.

In politics, also, new developments have arisen out of these fifty years of experience. When the Kuomintang arrived from the mainland, it imposed an authoritarian regime for quite some time. But within the KMT lay the seed of Sun Yat-sen's Three Principles of the People, and that seed was bound to put forth shoots, to bud, to flower, and finally to bear fruit. During the years under President Chiang Kai-shek, Taiwan's government was authoritarian in nature, but at that juncture it would have been next to impossible to introduce full-fledged democratic freedoms and institutions.

For one thing, on the mainland there was the seemingly invincible communist regime, though with hindsight we can now see that the various social reform campaigns that the regime forcibly carried out did nothing but wreak chaos and destruction. To understand the Chiang Kai-shek era, we need to look at it in context of conditions in China and throughout Asia at the time, rather than seeing it only in terms of a regime in exile from the mainland.

### Chiang Ching-kuo's School of Politics

It was the Chiang Ching-kuo regime that spanned the eras, letting Taiwan's history pass from his father's time to the present. All I can say is that it must have been historical necessity that cast Chiang Ching-kuo in particular in the role of bridge builder.

Shortly after his father married Soong Mei-ling, the young Chiang Ching-kuo went off to study communism in the Soviet Union. Put into the context of his later policies in Taiwan, this period of study in the U.S.S.R. was clearly of tremendous importance.

Despite having gone with high hopes to the U.S.S.R. to study the communist revolution, Chang Ching-kuo's expectations were dashed by the terrible hardships he encountered there. It seems unthinkable, but he was even sent to a labor camp in Siberia, which plunged him into a period of severe intellectual and psychological crisis. I am convinced it was this experience in the U.S.S.R. that made Chiang Ching-kuo a very different leader from his father in political style and direction.

Many times I was awed just by being in the presence of Chiang Ching-kuo, but I remember one occasion in particular. At the time he was premier (head of the Executive Yuan) and had just discovered that a relative who was a government official was guilty of corrupt dealings. He ordered that the man be given more than fifteen years in jail. Chiang Kai-shek is said to have remarked, "This time, Ching-kuo, your punishment is too severe." As I see it, the way Chiang Ching-kuo handled the incident demonstrated firm resolve and a willingness to act without hesitation.

Unquestionably, Chiang Ching-kuo was a statesman to the core. Compared with him, I was nothing but a greenhorn academic. But when he appointed me minister without portfolio, he knew I would do my best to formulate plans for the future well-being of Taiwan. Indeed, whenever we had important meetings on policy, I made a point of always having a proposal ready to submit for discussion.

At those times Chiang, who chaired the meetings, would carefully listen to my proposal and at the same time begin the responses that would eventually lead toward the outcome he wanted. The way he managed this process was skillful and sure, displaying the arts of a master politician. By comparing my own conclusions (presented at the meetings in the form of proposals) with Chiang's and analyzing the differences between them, I received my education in government. Gradually I was able to understand why Chiang Ching-kuo would come to a different conclusion from mine, and what political considerations I had failed to incorporate into my arguments.

I was a minister without portfolio for six years under Chiang Ching-kuo. Whenever he chaired a meeting I experienced a state of heightened tension, but those meetings turned out to be my instruction in government. If I really did grow from a mere theorist into a political leader, I give all the credit to my six years in Chiang Ching-kuo's "school of politics."

## Birth of a Liberal Democracy

Economically, the Chiang Ching-kuo era laid the foundations for the rapid development that was to follow. Politically, it provided the runway for popular sovereignty, in the true sense of the word, to take full flight later on. The Chiang Ching-kuo years gave us a time to nurture the kind of political leaders, myself included, who would meet the needs of succeeding generations.

In March 1996, when I was elected to be the ninth-term president of the ROC, Taiwan was in political transition. The job of president was not something I had inherited from someone else: I had been chosen for it by the people themselves by direct popular vote.

As long as I live I will never forget my inaugural day, May 20, 1996. Following a suggestion by my wife, Tseng Wen-fui, the ceremony opened with the "Ode to Joy" from Beethoven's Ninth Symphony, as an expression of my gratitude to the people.

For me it was a moment of jubilation when all of Taiwan's history and politics seemed to radiate in a sunburst of joy, ushering in the start of an era of new promise. In my inaugural address, I said:

> This gathering today does not celebrate the victory of any candidate, or any political party, for that matter. It honors a triumph of democracy for 21 million people. It salutes the con-

firmation of freedom and dignity—the most fundamental human values—in the Taiwan, Pescadores, Quemoy and Matsu area.

. . .

We in Taiwan have realized the Chinese dream. The Chinese of the twentieth century have been striving for the realization of a happy, wealthy China and of Dr. Sun Yat-sen's "popular sovereignty" ideal. For fifty years, we have created in the Taiwan, Pescadores, Quemoy, and Matsu area an eye-catching "economic miracle" and achieved world-acclaimed democratic reform.

Undoubtedly, some citizens of advanced countries take freedom, democracy, and human rights so much for granted that they find nothing especially impressive in what we had done. They should think back over the long history that brought them from feudalism to the point where they are now. They then would appreciate the historic significance of our accomplishment in building a democracy. They should remember, moreover, that Taiwanese have had to wage a constant struggle to ward off the threat from mainland China even as they strove to realize democracy.

## Foundation Laid by the Chiangs

I have gone back over Taiwan's experience here not out of nostalgia but to emphasize my recognition of the accumulated achievements that form the base of our lives today and to reiterate my conviction that our future is etched in the solid accomplishments of the present. Anything I have been able to contribute as president, moreover, has been made possible by my predecessors' contributions: Sun Yat-sen, whose ideas embedded in the Three Principles of the People have always inspired me; President Chiang Kai-shek, who ably defended Taiwan; and President Chiang Ching-kuo, who built the foundation for economic and political development.

In the historical record of the last half-century in Taiwan, it may appear that my pursuit of democratization marks a clear break with the past. Certainly that is not the case. The two Chiang governments probably appear starkly authoritarian by comparison, but had it not been for the foundations they laid, the Taiwan we see today might never have come into being.

Without the resilient leadership they provided during the past several decades, we can be almost certain that the Chinese Communist Party would have taken control of Taiwan. Then we, too, would have had to trudge the long and miserable road that our fellow compatriots in the mainland have followed.

History is filled with curious digressions and contradictions, but perhaps such a process is necessary. In our case, if you take the long view, it is the very junctures that seem to be regressive that turn out to be the pillars supporting us today.

I hold the accomplishments of the two former President Chiangs in highest esteem. It is they who built the base on which we now stand and from which we must now seek our political future. It would be a grave mistake to refuse to learn from them and do nothing but criticize, just as it would be ridiculous to say, "Lee Teng-hui, you're wrong to move away from the policies of your predecessors."

## Qualifications for the President in 2000

The future of the people of Taiwan, too, will be built upon all the efforts they have made until now. The "new Taiwanese" who will create a new Taiwan include the original indigenous people, those whose ancestors came here four hundred years ago, and those who arrived only recently. Anyone who lives in and loves Taiwan is a "new Taiwanese." Thus, the political leaders the "new Taiwanese" choose should be people who appreciate what has gone into the formation of Taiwan and can utilize what has been achieved so far.

On account of the 1988 election, Taiwan has been buzzing with speculation about the presidential election of 2000, the year my term runs out. Some people expect me to run again, but I will be seventy-seven in 2000 and do not plan to run anymore. The new president must be someone who can usher in a new era supported by the "new Taiwanese."

It is true that I have redirected the KMT to suit the changing times. Since the KMT is already more than eighty years old itself, I realized that adjustments were necessary to enable the party to respond to new developments, and so I made those accommodations. As a result, the KMT is now one of the oldest ruling political parties in existence. In the final analysis, the KMT is a rare case, a political party that has come through phases of authoritarianism, dictatorship, and democratization, and in the process has acquired a deep pool of experience.

I hope that those who lead the KMT in the future will learn and absorb the lessons of that history. Those who will guide

Taiwan's future must identify with the richness and variety that lie in its political heritage

If they do, then the experience of past leaders will be kept alive, their efforts will bear fruit, and the new leaders will have ready resources in tackling the challenges of the new era. This historical succession in leadership is what gives Taiwan's politics its continuity and its fund of wisdom, without which Taiwan might never have survived the sensitive and difficult period of the past five decades.

I ask the new president to study thoroughly and deeply. I ask him or her to understand the politics of a dangerous time when, with the threat from the mainland hanging over Taiwan, the government could hardly avoid being authoritarian. Finally, I hope to see the emergence of a president who is innovative, able, and willing to take on new challenges.

## National Science

One thing we can be certain of in Taiwan's future is the central place of economic policy. Our democratization process had its foundation on economic development. Indeed, economic development is the central pillar supporting Taiwan's very existence. It is imperative, therefore, to build a strong base for development, and that base is a citizenry with a solid grounding in science.

Having a sustained interest in the directions science is moving, for some time I have been buying and reading books published in Japan and other countries. I also try to obtain the latest science-related books from Japan to keep abreast of new developments and inventions.

As I see it, the key scientific field today is cognitive science, which is based on four other scientific disciplines: linguistics, psychology, neurology, and information science. Research on the brain has made enormous strides recently, revealing the chemical and physical structure of the brain to a degree that was inconceivable just a short time ago. In the quest to understand human thought, we are seeing many new interdisciplinary fields opening up, giving us a better comprehension of how the brain functions.

The work of these cutting-edge sciences is going to have a great impact on education. Especially in Taiwan, how the orientation of education is determined and incorporated into the curriculum has an important bearing on our children and their future.

The human brain is unbelievably complex, but with sophisticated electronic means of imaging available today, it can be observed in great detail. Scientists have even been able to discover how discrete parts of the brain function. This research, using analysis based on CAT (computer-axial tomography) scans, indicates that many parts of the brain in an average person are left unused. It appears, in other words, that while everyone has different abilities, there may also be many cases when poor development in certain parts of the brain is the result of inadequate or distorted education.

I believe that the latest research in these fields has important implications for the future. If we do not provide our children with the kind of education that will allow their varied abilities to blossom, what hope can we have for the development of Taiwan? I have been encouraging research on education for the future with emphasis on science, an approach I call "national science."

## Meeting of Minds

Golf is one of my favorite activities, but recently my game has suffered a horrendous slump. Trying to figure out what was wrong, I decided it was not a problem related to my general health but to a sudden worsening of my eyesight.

As my vision deteriorated I lost the ability to gauge distances accurately. Still, I went on swinging my driver as before and ended up misjudging, making shots that went wild. I could, of course, have simply blamed it on old age, but I realized that there was another lesson in this experience. In whatever shape or form, people have to try to understand the correlation between perceptions and actions in order to come up with correct judgments.

Later I told my physician about my abysmal golf game, trying out my theory on him that first your eyesight goes bad, then the brain misjudges the information it receives, sending the wrong signals to the hands, which proceed to work inadequately, the upshot being that the score on your golf card goes from bad to terrible. The doctor listened patiently and then responded, "Your theory makes sense!"

It is a small matter if you're only talking about an old man's game of golf. However, if such a series of misjudgments regularly influences children's education, its effectiveness will be seriously impaired.

I had heard that Bill Gates, chairman of Microsoft, was avidly developing something he called a digital nervous system, and so when he came to visit me, I was eager to hear more about this interest of his. There is a wide gap in our ages, but Bill and I got along well from the start.

Such was my amazement when I found in talking to him that what he was describing was almost exactly the same as my thoughts about "national science." The basic concepts form the field of cognitive science that is now standing at an intersection with information science, which involves computers, and brain science, which is attempting to tackle questions about the human psyche.

He laughed when I quipped, "Bill, I think you've been getting your ideas from my 'national science' model!" Of course I was joking, but it felt good to know that Bill Gates agreed that the general thrust of "national science" was on target.

### My Long Acquaintance with Computers

Today information science is hitting its stride, and not just in finance and communications. It is being applied wherever there is a need for more refined ways to think systematically, and in areas like public administration and education it is creating a veritable revolution.

My own use of computers dates from way back. When I was drafted into the military as a student during the Pacific War and sent to Chiba in Japan as a commissioned officer, I was put in charge of antiaircraft guns and used my free time to study mathematics. And math later helped me master statistics, which is essential in econometrics. During my first stay in the United States, when I was studying at Iowa State University, I had to master statistics in order to do research in my field, which was agricultural economics. I began by learning how to use a computer. It goes without saying that computers are an absolute necessity for performing complex calculations in econometrics.

Many, many years later, when I was mayor of Taipei, I brought computers into information processing in city government. We were the first in Taiwan to use computers in public administration.

The use of automobiles in Taiwan was spreading so quickly at that time that the police were unable to handle all the accident cases that kept pouring in. They were swamped, and probably because they resented the overload, at one point they stopped processing accident data altogether.

I had a serious talk with the chief of the city police about the danger of such negligence and gave him three months to get back on track in dealing with traffic violations and accidents. "If you can't manage this," I said, "I'll ask you to resign and bring in someone who can." He flew into action, of course, but he had no idea where to begin. He asked me for advice on how to change the system, and I suggested simply and concretely, "Why don't you try using computers."

It was also during my tenure as mayor that Taipei began using computers to tally the results in elections of representatives to the National Legislature. The polls closed at 5:00 P.M., and whereas the other districts could not finish counting until the following morning, Taipei alone was able to announce its figures by 8:30 the same night. The speed of our operation amazed the media commentators.

Again, when I was vice-president under Chiang Ching-kuo, I used any extra time I had to study new technologies. I wanted to know more about the latest research in areas like electronic sensor technology, microelectronics, and computer science. Aware that the level of Taiwan's industry could be improved with new technology, I set out to find out about what kind of technology would be both feasible and appropriate for them. That was yet another period of intensive study for me.

## Four Major Projects for the Twenty-first Century

Partly because I had been keeping up with advances in these areas, I had predicted early on that electronics and computerization would take off, as indeed they have, and I am neither surprised nor daunted by such innovations. The problem now is to determine what Taiwan's relative advantages are and in what areas it can become a leader in the region.

At present Taiwan's special strengths lie in manufacturing. I think that for some time, at least, we can maintain our comparative advantage in manufacturing. It is very possible that Taiwan could become the center of manufacturing industries in the Asia–Pacific region, with the core being microelectronics.

The areas where growth is gradually beginning to level off are the smokestack industries like steel and petrochemicals. This pattern is very familiar to Japanese, for during the half-century since World War II, their industry has undergone the same kind of change.

What, then, are Taiwan's challenges from now on? I believe there are four major ones: first, finance; second, satellite communications; third, airports; and fourth, ports. Anglo-Saxon countries now have overwhelming dominance in the first two areas. Many people are convinced that even Japan cannot break in very far. Yet it is just that type of pessimistic thinking that may make it possible for Taiwan to get a foot in the door.

I have doubts that Hong Kong will be able to maintain its role as a world financial center. Once Tokyo's financial market rebounds, it will no doubt become a center of global trading. What Taiwan offers as a financial center, on the other hand, are its potentially favorable qualifications to function as a center for the Asia–Pacific region. The foundations are there in strong economic development and social stability. Taiwan also has a well-educated population and is equipped with advanced technology. These conditions are all in place.

Taiwan is also building communications satellites. There must be ten or fifteen in orbit to create a network evenly covering the globe. With a Chinese-oriented media network of this kind we could bring together the 1.3 billion Chinese-speaking people scattered all over the world. Taiwan is in a good position to take the initiative in creating just such a Chinese-language network.

Finally, Taiwan has numerous geographical advantages that could be utilized for airport and harbor development. To name a few projects that are already under way, Chiang Kai-shek International Airport and the Kaoshiung Harbor will be completely rebuilt and incorporated into new city planning schemes. In addition, with plans for developing other new ports, Taiwan is preparing to become a regional center for air and sea transportation. Thus, while the steel and petrochemical industries are in a slow decline, we can nonetheless be certain that Taiwan's exports and imports will only grow from now on.

## More Power to Agriculture

Despite the attention we are giving to new industries and other frontiers, we have by no means forgotten about agriculture, Taiwan's economic cornerstone. To recapitulate, I have pushed for agricultural reform, and my basic position has remained the same: agriculture cannot be treated as a separate problem divorced from other vital sectors, and we must not allow farmland to become the object of speculation. Many problems remain, however.

"Core farm households," which were created by the land reforms, have had a very hard time increasing productivity, mainly because of the small scale of their operations and limited financial resources. In fact, while other sectors have used technological innovation to achieve prodigious leaps in productivity, core farm households are constantly concerned about being left behind.

One view is that the core farm households ought to be incorporated, but we must be very careful. Once they become agricultural corporations, someone is bound to begin thinking of ways to make them more viable financially, and before you know it such efforts will have turned into speculation in farmland by commercial businesses. As soon as farmland is bought up by such enterprises, it gets turned into residential land, is subdivided and sold, or it is scooped up and converted before you know it into luxury dwellings.

If nothing is done about the less productive farmland, those fields are going to be used by other industries with higher productivity. When that happens, agriculture in Taiwan will go into decline, no matter what we do to sustain it. We can incorporate farms, thereby allowing them to secure sufficient funds, but that approach will help solve the problem only if the farms devote their resources to the development and maintenance of agriculture.

Agriculture in Taiwan has to make the effort to adopt new technology and become self-sustaining. We could, for example, introduce satellite exploration technology as a means to improve agricultural land; exploit solar energy to cut down on fuel costs; reduce labor costs by making use of robotic tractors; apply genetic engineering to improve crop strains, and so forth. Those are only some of the possibilities, but they raise yet another problem: the more technology is exploited, the greater the demand for funds and technical know-how.

Venture capital in agriculture may be the most reliable means to ensure that such a transition goes smoothly. The various research projects now under way have to be applied to agriculture on a continuing basis, and that requires funds and incentives to encourage actual implementation on the farm. The problems of agriculture are not going to be solved simply by more advanced technology or higher productivity.

## Parliamentary Reform

We can be certain that industry in twenty-first-century Taiwan will develop around new technology and new systems and procedures, but what about politics and society? Our political and social systems and institutions should be improved and changed to something better than those we have now.

One of my current priorities is parliamentary reform. Until now Taiwan has had three parliamentary bodies, which are the National Assembly, the Legislature, and the Provincial Assembly. Before the 1990s there had been virtually no new blood in the National Assembly since its founding, while the Legislature was almost completely ineffectual. What most Taiwanese associated with the word "parliament," however, was the Provincial Assembly, which is not even a national-level institution.

The streamlining and reorganization of the Provincial Government as an administrative unit under the Executive Yuan has already been decided, and so the function of the Provincial Assembly will be taken over by the National Legislature. And with the restructuring of the National Assembly and the Legislature, we will help rid the system of fictitious, overlapping, and conflicting functions and provide new institutions that are democratic in both name and performance.

Of course some legislators are bound to insist that such restructuring is unnecessary. Yet in the general election of December 1998, the people gave solid support to my call for parliamentary reform. In my mind, the proposed reform, along with judicial and educational reforms, is a priority item on the agenda to be accomplished before the twenty-first century.

The kind of education people receive, the kind of legal system that governs their society, and the kind of parliamentary institutions through which the popular will is reflected form the tripod on which democracy rests. All three have to be clearly structured, streamlined, and operational. However, if the people do not have a deep understanding of their full significance, in no way can that nation be called "democratic." I am absolutely determined to carry out these three monumental reforms before the end of my term. I can then step down with great hopes for the future.

## Defense for Survival

Besides our continuing economic prosperity and ongoing political reforms, we have to consider the special defense needs of Taiwan. We can widen Taiwan's network of economic ties, and through pragmatic foreign relations raise its international status, but if we neglect its military, it may not survive. That is the simple reality of Taiwan today.

We are now laying the groundwork for revising the national defense law and laws governing the organization of the defense forces. These are also tied up with the democratization program. Formerly, there were no specific stipulations concerning defense. For all practical purposes, the president made decisions about defense by himself and had them carried out as he directed.

The revisions provide for a new defense law, which removes some authority over the three branches of the military from the president and delegates it to the minister of defense. Furthermore, whereas the chief of staff used to have to answer only to the president in military affairs, the new law will change that and clarify the relationship between the minister of defense and the chief of staff, giving the latter more jurisdiction over matters concerning military operations.

Organizationally, the biggest problem has been a top-heavy military proportionately overloaded with generals relative to the numbers in the lower ranks. We need to reduce the number of generals and restore a reasonable balance to the corps.

The military has been organized around divisions, each division consisting of 5,000 troops, which is too small; normally a unit that is any smaller than 10,000 is not called a division. We plan, therefore, to reorganize on the basis of brigades instead of divisions, to abolish the rank of division commander, and to clearly demarcate the chain of command.

In view of the types of wars that erupt today, it makes sense to use brigades as the main units, for they have the necessary flexibility in complicated military maneuvers. Military units nowadays are no longer simple organizations. We still need infantry, of course, but we also need tank corps and then, for cover, air corps. On top of that, modern warfare involves many special technical corps as well.

Once you try to put all the above into a single organization, the whole body works more slowly and its effectiveness is dulled. The best option is to organize by function, to some extent by creating separate tank brigades, helicopter brigades, and so forth, and then when military action is called for, bring the several brigades together.

There is also the problem of weapons and corruption. The

more advanced military technology becomes, the more easily graft creeps into ordnance procurement. Taiwan's defense budget has no margin for waste. It must be allocated carefully and effectively. For that reason, I believe we must be uncompromising toward corruption in defense contracts and very strict in punishing offenders.

## Adequate Social Security

For the Taiwan of tomorrow, an adequate social security system will be a categorical imperative. In this rapidly changing world, social problems are bound to arise that are beyond the capacity of individual citizens to cope with. For Taiwan, I see two major problems emerging as our society undergoes change.

The first concerns social security for the aborigines. Taiwan's national wealth has increased very rapidly, but some of our people have not yet been able to share in that affluence. In the case of the indigenous people, they lost the base for their traditional lifestyles but failed to adapt to another way of life.

Actually there are very few countries in the world that have found satisfactory ways to resolve this problem. Democracy presumes the equality of all people, but as a capitalist economy expands, such minorities, people who have been detached from their former ways of life, are not necessarily given acceptable alternatives. Think of African-Americans and the struggle they have had, or the poor whites in the American south. Clearly this problem is unimaginably difficult.

In Taiwan, our goal, as expressed by the "new Taiwanese" concept, is to provide everyone with the same opportunities. We plan to formulate a financial assistance policy for the indigenous people to pursue economic prosperity while holding on to their ancient cultures. This process will take time and patience.

The second is a problem all advanced countries are facing to one degree or another—the aging society. The rate of increase in the senior population is the most rapid in Japan. Although Taiwan's aging population is not rising as quickly as in Japan, the same situation looms not far ahead.

In practical terms, larger numbers of elderly people will require expanded medical facilities and more homes for the aged. We can learn a great deal by studying how the industrial countries are responding to the needs of the growing population of old people. On the one hand, the deep current of Chinese culture in Taiwan has instilled an almost instinctive sense of respect for one's parents, yet the number of families where parents and married children live together is, nonetheless, rapidly dwindling. I think we can expect to see the same kinds of problems in Taiwan's aging society that are now emerging in the West and Japan.

Our government has begun to address this issue. One proposal is to expand the geriatric units in those public hospitals that used to be under the jurisdiction of the provincial government. The Bureau of Health has approved this proposal and is now drafting a working plan, which ought to be completed very soon.

When I was mayor of Taipei, I was solidly behind the construction of an old people's home, which Taiwanese refer to as "homes of peaceful comfort." It was built as a joint government–

private sector project. As long as private funds are involved in a project, it has to be run as a business, so the facilities are better. It was successful enough that others like it were built later in each of Taiwan's counties, with three in Taipei alone.

We are now also planning an old-age pension system for farmers and low-income city dwellers, using money they pay in. Together with the national pension fund, which goes into effect in 2000, we will have completed one link in a policy for our aging society.

Certainly, social welfare is important, but the amount of welfare provided must be weighed against its burden on society. The countries of northern Europe are an obvious case in point. Having to supply excessive amounts of welfare and social security, they have raised taxes, and that has drained some vitality from their societies. There will be hard questions to face: How far is the government responsible? And how much of the burden should individuals shoulder, and in what form?

A substantial social security system is very important, and we intend to do everything possible to meet this challenge, but money alone cannot solve all welfare issues. In the final analysis, the difficulties experienced by minorities and the anxiety and unhappiness of elderly citizens are often related to loss of confidence, of peace of mind, and of a sense of security. Money is never a panacea.

## Promoting Cultural Activities
People never stop wishing for beauty, elegance, and freshness in their lives. They seek something beyond material affluence. When

I think about what I want for Taiwan, apart from any economic, political, and social agenda, I always come back to the same thing—art and culture. And here, too, I think we have laid a solid foundation for the future.

When I was mayor, I took my wife's suggestion that we organize a music festival. At first it was just a music program, but then we added drama and it became a festival of arts. Though somewhat extravagant at the time, it was a great success. It included a performance of Goethe's *Faust*, which I personally translated into Chinese in 1981. The festival is still held regularly in Taipei.

After my appointment as president, I decided to use Chieh Shou Hall, which is located within the Presidential Office, for a new concert series. We invite musicians from Taiwan and other countries in Asia to perform. For them, these concerts provide a good opportunity to play before sophisticated audiences. Some of the musicians are rising young stars, but many others are amateurs. The audience includes schoolteachers, businesspeople, and people from the countryside whose hobby is music. Chieh Shou Hall continues to be Taiwan's musical mecca to this day.

When I started the music festival, I also initiated another program in the schools. The primary schools instituted special music classes, and children in the classes with outstanding musical talent were offered the opportunity for further training. Today there is a special budget set aside for music training for junior high and high school students as well.

Now the government offers scholarships to students with talent to study music abroad. The results of the program are already apparent in the growing number of young Taiwanese who are making their mark internationally. Most of them are products of our music program for the gifted.

Taiwan presently has a fine arts college and an academy of art, and there are proposals afoot to build a separate college of music and a music academy. There is tremendous enthusiasm for these plans, and I want to support them in every way I can.

Naturally, the support of music education and training of musicians is only a small part of Taiwan's whole program in the arts. We are encouraging rich artistic expression by citizens in other fields as well; we are nurturing an appreciation of beauty among our people and continuing to provide an environment for the development of culture in all its richness and depth. It gives me tremendous pleasure to know that by starting music education, I made a contribution to the way the arts are blossoming in Taiwan today.

## When Lee Teng-hui Leaves

There is not much left of this century, which means that the day when I leave office is fast approaching. I realize that people think of me as having made Taiwan a prosperous, democratic land, but actually at the outset I never envisioned myself in this role. Not once could I have imagined becoming a politician, much less president.

No, I am not a born statesman, but one thing I know is that I have always had a deep love for Taiwan. It may sound arrogant to say that in my devotion to this land I am second to none, but deep within I think that feeling was what woke me to what I wanted to do. That powerful feeling has sustained me through my ever-changing life, sometimes burning with fierce determination, other times perking quietly and tranquilly, but for seventy-odd years it has never left me. Sometimes when I think of what Taiwan has become, I feel like shouting Goethe's matchless line, "Ah, tarry still! Thou art so fair!" Yet Taiwan still has many challenges to meet and many trials to undergo. The history of Taiwan is still being written.

When I spoke of my political philosophy, I noted that a true leader has to think about what will happen when he is absent; what kind of judgments will others make when he is not there to lead them? That is precisely what I must think about now: "Taiwan without Lee Teng-hui." What will happen in Taiwan after I leave office?

Comparing Taiwan and Singapore, Professor Samuel Huntington, the American political scientist, predicted that Taiwan's democracy will almost certainly endure even after Lee Teng-hui dies, but with the death of Lee Kuan Yew the basic foundation of the political system he built in Singapore may go with him.

Lee Kuan Yew is my friend and I have only the highest admiration for his political leadership, and so I had very mixed thoughts about those words. Yet I have to admit that when I compare the political developments and cultures of Taiwan and Singapore, I think Huntington's intuition captured an essential difference.

A politician's actions are affected by the constraints of the stage where he or she appears. Regardless of whether or not Lee Kuan Yew might have wished for a place like Taiwan, his arena was Singapore, a smaller place cut through by complex international political forces.

From the beginning of this volume I have spoken of how greatly times have changed; now, instead of lamenting the "pathos of being born Taiwanese," we rejoice in the "good fortune of being Taiwanese." As a Taiwanese, I have been blessed to have this land as my stage where, for several decades, I have given my utmost and done everything in my power for the sake of Taiwan. If Professor Huntington is right, my efforts will endure in this beautiful land even after I am gone. In this, too, I am blessed with the "good fortune of being born Taiwanese."

# *Afterword*

IN THIS book, while I have said all that I wish to say at present, there are two points which I would like to further elaborate.

One concerns what I believe to be the positive, affirmative view of life. As I wrote in the pages above, I have been torn throughout my life between a fierce urge for complete affirmation of the ego, on the one hand, and a strong determination to somehow control and negate that ego, on the other; for many years of my life I could not seem to maintain a proper balance.

I realize, however, that this struggle is by no means unique to me. The clash of contradictory urges besets all young people and challenges every human being in the course of living. It is the imbalance between the egotistical urge and the will to overcome the ego that has thrown contemporary society into disequilibrium; indeed, I believe the failure to find that balance is the fundamental cause of the crisis of civilizations in our world today.

Drawing from my own experience, I have taken every opportunity to encourage young people to discard self-centered thinking and free themselves from attachment to the past. As long as you adopt a self-centered view in your thinking and cling to the past, you cannot achieve a positive, forward-looking attitude toward life.

I have found, moreover, that positive thinking and the ability to let go of the past are two sides of the same coin. If either one is missing, balance cannot be achieved and one becomes obsessed with an unresolvable conflict between self-centeredness and self-denial. When I turned twenty, I made up my mind to cease keeping a diary. The custom of keeping a diary is usually considered admirable, but it can also become a bad habit. I say this because, for a person who is intensely self-conscious, a diary can either become a device of self-aggrandizement or pit of endless reflection and self-reproach. At one point, my diary became a liturgy of contrition and regrets. It is important, of course, to be able to see yourself critically and to reflect on what you have done, but soul-searching alone will not help you get through life. At the same time, we need the capacity to move on, to overcome the odds, and to look to the future.

What happened after I gave up writing my diary? I was able, at least, to escape the proclivity for excessive self-absorption that had plagued my youth. Ultimately, it was only after my encounter with Christianity that I was truly freed from the inner face-off between egotism and altruism. Put the other way around, I was able to embrace Christianity because it allowed me to deal with the inner contradictions I had previously struggled in vain to resolve.

The moment that is addressed by Christianity is what one might call "reversal of the order of the self and the other." The most important aspect of this teaching is embracing the God within each of us. By recognizing the inner spirit of God that forgives others through profound love, our tendency to self-centeredness dissipates, and the spirit of love and care to others flourishes.

Put in a fashion more accessible to the young, perhaps, it is the same as saying that people with a very strong sense of self need to shift their thinking from that centering on themselves as individuals to that revolving around the concerns of their society. By incorporating one's need for self-affirmation into an outlook centered on society, the will and the passion to work for society and for its people will emerge.

I believe that the same principle applies to all the problems that plague modern-day society. Even in the advanced industrial nations, these derive, on the one hand, from people's uncontrolled desires and greed, and on the other, from their stubborn rejection of the constraints of society. Taiwan's society still betrays the toll exacted by this imbalance, and it is for this reason that I believe we must endeavor to achieve a "spiritual revitalization" before it is too late.

The "self-affirming world view" that I have advocated, I repeat, is not the embrace of untrammeled egotism. On the contrary, we need a world view that we can be confident will both restrain the excesses of wanton egotism and arrest the pervasive decay of social mores. The self-affirmation I advocate is that which affirms others through the exercise of self-denial and which represents a pure-minded commitment to the future.

The second point I would like to add concerns my wife, Tseng

Wen-fui. Although not mentioned in detail in the text, I would not have been involved in political life as I am today nor have come to think as I do today if it had not been for her presence. Without her support, I would not have been able to rise above the nihilism I confronted in my intellectual quest for answers to life's questions and would not have survived the cruel terrorism of the late 1940s. She was the one who introduced me to Christianity and who encouraged me to be baptized.

If I had been alone when I faced the need for the solace of religion and found myself frustrated by an overpowering sense of a philosophical gridlock, it is unlikely that I would have responded to the idea of God's love or accepted baptism.

As I have said, despite the breadth of my study and reading, I found it very difficult to accept anything on faith. While visiting churches around Taiwan over several years, I struggled alone to know the nature of faith and enter the realm of the faithful. Of course, faith is not something that can be rationally understood. I was able to understand faith through the companionship of my loving wife and family.

For me, the most painful aspect of my career is not so much the risk to my life that it sometimes involves but rather the danger posed to my wife and family because of my political activities. In the course of our movement for democratization we faced great opposition and suffered serious slander and threats to our lives.

As the elections for president approached, I urged Tseng Wen-fui many times to leave Taiwan and await the results in another country. I have always been ready to endure whatever cost I had to pay for my political convictions, but I find it intolerable to watch my wife suffer because of my ideas. Although I hesitate to say so, my wife and children have endured countless slander and intimidation on my behalf. I have often regretted for their sake that I have chosen this career in politics.

I would like, therefore, to express herein my deep gratitude and respect for my life's partner, Tseng Wen-fui. Without her faithful encouragement and support through the years, I could not have withstood life's tempestuous storms.

# *Index*

humanism (*jenpen*) 43
Huntington, Samuel 218–19

*I Ching* (The Book of Changes) 42–44;
  the principle of *i* (change) 42–43
Ito, Kiyoshi 129

Japan 77; as a guide 85–87; "core-
  satellite" organization 86–87;
  economy 142–44; fiscal deficit
  143–44; Japanese-style management 87; the media 135, 141;
  politicians, hereditary tendency 80;
  politics 145–46, 157–58; revision of
  the Constitution 152; security
  150–51; small-group activity 86;
  strong points 148

Kissinger, Henry 79
Kuo, Mo-juo 29
Kuomintang (KMT, Nationalist
  Party) 20, 35, 36, 92, 124; relocation
  of the capital to Taiwan 37
Kurata, Hyakuzo 26
Kyoto Imperial University 21

land 46–48; reform 47
Lee, Chiang-chin 21, 23–24
Lee, Chin-lung 21–23
liberal democracy 70–72, 98
Lu, Hsun 29

Ma, Ying-jeou 191–92
Mao, Zedong 33–34
Marx, Karl 31–33; Marxist economics
  35
Miyazawa Plan 176
Motoori, Norinaga 27

name, doctrine of 28
National Assembly 92, 93

National Security Council 92
National Taiwan University 21
nationalism: two types 61–62
Natsume, Soseki 26
Nietzsche 40
North Korea 174–75
Nye, Joseph 150; Nye Report 184

Obuchi, Keizo 99
one-China policy 119
"one country, two systems"
  formula 120–21

patience 65, 95, 118–19, 214
peasant revolution 33–34
People's Republic of China (PRC) 9,
  46, 120, 122, 125, 129–31, 140–41,
  169, 182
politicians 59, 80

Republic of China on Taiwan:
  definition of Taiwan's status 52, 181
Retrocession Day speech (Oct. 24,
  1998)
reunification 120–23
Rockefeller III, John D. 132
roundabout approach 65–70
Russia 151

saving face 29
Schultz, Theodore W. 48, 49
Shinran 26, 40
Shiomi, Kaoru 31
slogan (words) 28–29
Soros, George 169
speculation 169
spirit 105; crisis of 106; training 156–
  57
Sun Yat-sen 44, 46, 49, 61, 198; Three
  Principles of the People 44–46,
  75, 194; "The world is for all" 44,

46, 63–65
Suzuki, Daisetz 25
symbiotic community 61

Taipei mayoral election (Dec. 1998) 191
Taiwan Strait: "public assets" 183–84
Taiwan Sugar Corporation 111
Taiwan: agricultural reform 67, 208–09; agriculture 48–50, 103; conglomerates 90; consensus 110; Constitution 92; "core farming households" 68; defense 211–13; democracy 211; diversity 55; educational reforms 103–08; emergency mobilization 93; "existence" 95–98, 120, 181–82, 188; foreign relations 95–98; foreign workers 127; government monopoly 101; identity 51–52; import of agricultural products 102; judicial reform 108–10; meat market 102; medical care insurance system 74–75; music festival 216; new center of Chinese culture 31, 43, 60, 62–63; "new Taiwanese" 61, 191–94, 200, 213; parliamentary reform 210–11; "permanent" parliament 92; popular sovereignty 60; privatization of state enterprises 87; "quiet revolution" 126; school textbooks 107–108; social security 213–15; "Taiwan experience" 109, 123–28; Taiwanese organizations overseas connected via Internet 133–34; telecommunications business 88; welfare 54; workers training 89;
Temporary Provisions Effective During the Period of National Mobilization for Suppression of the Communist Rebellion ("Temporary Provision") 74, 91–93
Thurow, Lester C. 71–73
Toyota Motors 100
"turnpike theory" 66, 69

United States: as guide 78–78; China policy 79; Congress 79, 130–31; foreign policy 79; global standards 99; new world order 99; policy toward Taiwan 129–32; Taiwan Relations Act 129, 134; "three noes" policy 129–31

*Wall Street Journal* article (August 3, 1998) 53–54
welfare 44–45, 75
West Virginia 132
Wittfogel, Karl 33
World Trade Organization 101

Zen: concept of self-control 25